Travels in Southern California

1. *John Xántus*, lithograph by Giuseppi Marastoni, 1862. Portrait Collection of the Austrian National Library

Travels in
Southern California

by

John Xántus

translated and edited by
Theodore Schoenman
and Helen Benedek Schoenman

with an Introduction by Theodore Schoenman

Wayne State University Press   Detroit, 1976

Title of original edition: Utazás Kalifornia Déli Részeiben, Budapest,
1859.

Copyright © 1976 by Wayne State University Press,
Detroit, Michigan 48202. All rights are reserved.
No part of this book may be reproduced without formal permission.

Xántus, János, 1825–1894.
   Travels in southern California.

   Translation of Utazás Kalifornia déli részeiben.
   Bibliography: p.
   Includes index.
   1. California, Southern—Description and travel.
2. Baja California—Description and travel. 3. Xántus,
János, 1825–1894. I. Title.
F867.X213   917.94'9'044   76-23224
ISBN 0-8143-1570-4

to Edith

Contents

Illustrations and Maps

Acknowledgments

The illustrations and map are reproduced by courtesy of the Library Audiovisual and Photographic Services, University of California, Los Angeles, California.

We wish to express our appreciation to Elaine P. Halperin for her many pertinent suggestions and painstaking editing of the manuscript.

Introduction

When one enters the famous Zoo at Budapest, one comes face to face with the statue of John (János) Xántus (1825–1894). The inscription states that he was the founder and first director of the Zoo and Botanical Gardens. He was also curator of the ethnological section of the National Museum and his collections of North American and East Asian flora and fauna have gained a widespread reputation.

For his scientific achievements and ardent patriotism, which brought him well earned recognition, he was greatly honored; but his popular fame rested chiefly on having provided the literature of his native country with its first intimate knowledge of the western frontier in general, and the brawling, bouncing state of California (both Alta and Baja) in particular. He became widely known as a great adventurer and frontiersman, an explorer of the Wild West, and his two books recording his adventures solidly established his authority as a prime source of the geography, ethnology, and natural history of the North American west.

The general American public is largely unaware that this man spent but thirteen years in America, between 1851 and 1864 during which brief period he put American natural history permanently in his debt. Although ignored by historians, Xántus is well known to ornithologists, entomologists, coleopterists, botanists, and other natural

11

historians for his massive contributions in all these fields. The United States National Museum contains a wealth of zoological and botanical specimens collected by Xántus for the Smithsonian Institution.

In 1848, as a consequence of the French revolution, the Napoleonic era, the Vienna Congress, and the subsequent oppressive regime of Metternich, France, Germany, Italy and Hungary were a-blaze with social and political uprisings and revolutions. The result was that political exiles flocked to America, seeking refuge. Among these were two Hungarians whose accomplishments in their adopted land assured them an indelible page in our history. Both of them described their experiences in their native tongue and published them in their native country. The first was Agoston Haraszthy, who became known as the "father of California viticulture" and founded the giant California wine industry. The second was János Xántus, zoologist, botanist, or-nithologist, ethnologist, a man for all seasons in natural history.

The high value of Xántus's many years of uncompensated and faithful service to natural history cannot be overestimated.[1] His fellow scientists credit him with being perhaps our most noteworthy collector of naturalia. His prolific pioneering has widely broadened the know-ledge of such systematizers and technicians as Baird, Cassin, Lawrence, LeConte, Gray, Palmer,[2] and many others, about the entire biota of large regions of the west, then but little known. Some evidence of the high esteem accorded his activities are the tributes paid to him by fellow workers in the field.[3]

Xántus's emergence from total obscurity to eminence, and his pathfinding adventures in the trackless west are truly an exciting tale.

He was born on October 5, 1825, at Csokonya, county of Somogy, in the south of Hungary, the son of Ignacz, a superintendent and steward on the estate of Count Széchényi. Educated at the Benedictine gymnasium at Györ, he graduated in 1841. While studying for the bar, he served for three years as a county official of some importance. In 1847 he was admitted to the bar at Pest and returned to his birthplace to practice law. Undoubtedly he would have become a minor local officeholder had not the turbulent waves of the revolution of 1848 determined his ultimate fate. He enlisted enthusiastically in Kossuth's revolutionary army and fought in several battles, rising to the rank of first lieutenant in the infantry. When the war of independence was lost, he was taken prisoner by the victorious Austrians and imprisoned at the Königgrätz fortress in Bohemia. His mother's money managed to obtain his release; rather than return to his beloved but oppressed homeland, he joined a group of refugees in Dresden, Saxony, in July 1850, where Metternich's police spies took notes of his rousing, patriotic speeches. As he was attempting to visit his home, he was arrested in Prague and forced to serve as a private in the Austrian Army. He escaped on foot and reached safety in Saxony whence, via Hamburg, he was helped to reach London. On May 5, 1851, he sailed to the New World.

Xántus landed in New York with seven dollars in his pocket and spent the early years in America under precarious conditions. In his letters to his family he proudly admits working as a shop clerk, bookseller, druggist, piano teacher, as well as an instructor of German, French, and Spanish. Preferring not to take advantage of "high-placed" social connections, he was also a laborer, "digging ditches while standing in water waist high."

He was deeply attached to his family and wrote a series of tender letters, chiefly to his mother. The letters give a vivid and intimate account of his ceaseless efforts to advance his fortune, describe his daily routine, the itinerary of his wanderings, and include incisive comments on the astounding vitality of the new, emerging giant among the nations; his poignant observations about the lifestyle of the rising entrepreneur middle class, contrast sharply with the pitiable destiny of the many Indian tribes he befriended.

The thirty-seven letters cover the period from December 1, 1852, to July 5, 1857; they are dated from many points, extending from the Gulf of Mexico and New Orleans, to the Kansas and Nebraska Indian frontiers; from the pioneer Hungarian colonies of Iowa to Fort Riley and Fort Laramie; from the Canadian and Red Rivers to the Llano Estacado in Texas, Colorado, and Utah. His graphic descriptions of the large cities of the east—New York, Philadelphia, Washington—offer a colorful portrait of the contemporary urban scene, while the narrative of his journey to California via Panama and the rousing spectacle of San Francisco in the 1850s attest to his perceptive eye for significant detail.

These letters constitute Xántus's first book, published in 1858 in Pest, under the title *Letters from North America*.* The book also dis-

_____

*Trans. Theodore Schoenman and Helen Benedek Schoenman (Detroit: Wayne State University Press, 1975).

plays another facet of this unique pioneer of the frontier: his elaborate and constant deception about his true situation. He told his mother and family the story of heading an important railroad survey to plan the route from St. Louis to California and later commanding an expedition to search for the headwaters of the Arkansas River. He recounted fictitious tales about the various responsible positions he was holding and his grandiose plans for the future—all this while he was reduced "in a moment of utmost despair, and under circumstances completely beyond my control" to entering the American Army.[4]

Xántus enlisted in the United States Army at St. Louis on November 24, 1855, under the assumed name of Louis Vesey. He felt so degraded by this desperate step that he kept it a secret from his family. According to some records, he was assigned to the medical department but, to whatever branch of the service he may have been attached, it seems evident from his extensive and detailed account of this period that he was constantly in the field on the borders of Kansas Territory, engaged exclusively in boundary survey. Often he was detached from his regular duties as a topographic draftsman and put in command of exploring parties to map Indian territories seldom visited by a white man. These surveying expeditions were aimed at ascertaining the most practicable route for a railroad to pass from the Mississippi River to the Pacific Ocean, and they were under the supervision of the secretary of war. Xántus's pay was fifty dollars a month.

At Fort Riley, Kansas, which was the headquarters of Xántus's team, he attracted the attention of Dr. William A. Hammond (1828–1900), assistant surgeon of the Army, who later became one of the great surgeon-generals of the U.S. Army. Hammond, a devoted ornithologist, was one of the young officers aided and inspired by Professor Spencer Baird, the future secretary of the Smithsonian Institution. Hammond, quickly recognizing Xántus's natural bent and exceptional qualifications for natural history, guided and encouraged him in its pursuit. Their association resulted in Xántus's collection of a large quantity of flora and fauna as well as minerals which he sent to the Smithsonian Institution. Xántus stayed in Kansas Territory until about March 1857. During this period his personal collection included some 300 different snakes, 200 lizards, 700 fishes and forty boxes of plants which he ultimately presented to the Academy of Natural Sciences of Philadelphia, the Smithsonian Institution, and the National Museum of Hungary.

Xántus's name was becoming known in scientific circles. He was proposed for membership and elected to the Academy of Natural Sciences. The lowly enlisted man's feats are best judged by Baird's evaluation in his letter of recommendation to W. M. Seward, secretary of state, dated November 15, 1862: "Mr. Xantus is the most accomplished and successful explorer in the field of natural history I have ever known or ever heard of, the results of his operations enriching the Smithsonian Museum in a very high degree."

In the spring of 1857 Baird wished to utilize Xántus's talents in a region which was terra incognita from the standpoint of natural history, the great Central Valley of California and the Sierra Nevada. He arranged therefore for his transfer to Fort Tejon, California and at the same time sponsored his promotion to the rank of hospital steward (sergeant). Xántus traveled from Fort Riley to Washington, where he was received by President Buchanan, who inquired about his explorations and about the activities of Louis Kossuth. He continued on to Philadelphia to deliver his speech accepting membership in the Academy of Natural Sciences and finally to New York where he boarded the steamer *Illinois* on April 6 for Panama. He crossed the isthmus on a jungle train and sailed on *The Golden Gate* to San Francisco, where he arrived on April 29, 1857. In a letter he commented that this long journey took no longer than a trip by stage coach across Hungary.

Life in San Francisco was briskly sketched in his letters. He observed that everything was focused around gold and gold mining. Half the advertisements in the newspapers (seventeen in all) catered to the needs of gold miners, and one-third of their content dealt with gold quotations. The rest reported mostly murders and other crimes connected with gold. Xántus describes in minute detail a very modern gold refinery established by his illustrious countryman, the renowned "father of California viticulture," Agoston Haraszthy.

At this point Xántus's book ended, to be followed by the sequel, the present volume, *Travels in Southern California.*

After spending ten days in San Francisco, Xántus proceeded via San Pedro and Los Angeles to Fort Tejon, where he arrived on May 18, 1857. During his twenty-month stay at Fort Tejon, while still serving as a hospital steward, he worked in his spare time as a naturalist, and with such industry and effectiveness that he was able to collect a wealth of specimens on which important findings by all the leading eastern systematists were based. The collection he shipped to the Smithsonian consisted of twenty-four cases. Xántus accomplished this in the face of many irritating obstacles because, in spite of Baird's support, his commanding officer and other superiors tried to restrict him to the military post and would not permit him to hunt or explore the region. In his reports to Baird, Xántus bitterly complained about the antagonism and obstructionism of the military toward enlisted men.

Xántus's reputation for the excellence of his collections and for his scientific versatility grew apace and, as a partial reward, he was granted a discharge from the army and appointed tide observer for the United States Coast Survey. He was to carry out this assignment at Cape San Lucas, at the southernmost tip of the peninsula of Lower California. He was also committed to continue collecting for the Smithsonian Institution and so, on January 25, 1859, he left Fort Tejon for San Francisco, where he stayed until March 14 to prepare his equipment. He reached his post at Cape San Lucas on April 4, 1859, and stayed there until August 1861. During his tenure he explored the lower part of the peninsula, the adjacent islands in the Gulf of California, Tres Marias Islands, Mazatlan on the mainland, and other localities. His explorations were of such importance that he won the most extravagant praise from his fellow naturalists.[5]

His assignment in Baja California more or less completed, Xántus cast his eye on what he considered a position of honor, an appointment to the consular service. His mentor, Baird, was pulling strings in Washington to get his protégé the desired post. But this took time and in the end Xántus left Baja California without any definite promise of employment. He was not altogether disappointed, for nostalgia exerted a strong pull. Before making a final commitment about his future course, he was eager to visit his family, his old friends, and his homeland. The amnesty of 1859 opened the door for his return without fear of arrest and so, after twenty-eight months of fruitful labor at Cape San Lucas, he returned to San Francisco in August 1861 and, with stopovers in Panama, New York and Bremen, reached his home in November 1861. Not unexpectedly, he was lionized. His ornithological collection was prominently featured in the press; he was inaugurated before a large and distinguished audience as a member of the Hungarian Academy of Sciences, and his speech on the physical geography of the ocean was enthusiastically received. He also spent much of his time arranging and cataloguing the North American material in the National Museum. But the welcome he received did not deter him from returning to America to obtain a position of rank befitting his exploits. He landed in New York for the second time in July 1862. In Washington he called on his first protector and collaborator, Dr. William A. Hammond, who three months earlier had been appointed surgeon-general of the army. Hammond obtained a very unusual appointment: he had Xántus commissioned as acting assistant surgeon-general in spite of the fact that Xántus was not a physician. So Xántus was back in the organization he detested, the army; he served only briefly in this capacity, however, for his appointment as U.S. Consul at Manzanillo, on the west coast of Mexico, came through. His salary was to be $125 a month. Xántus sailed from New York in December 1862 with the good wishes of Baird, who in his report to the regents of the Smithsonian, wrote: "I doubt not that, with unabated zeal, he will be able to add much that is new and important to the different branches of natural history."[6]

At Manzanillo and Colima, where he established his consular office, Xántus continued his exacting explorations on the Pacific slope of the Sierra Madre, a new and mostly unexplored area of natural history. His consular duties were less than exacting and he frequently ventured off on field trips. He also got himself embroiled in an incident that led to his dismissal by the State Department. John S. Blake, an American mine operator, was subjected to continuous attacks and held for ransom by a local rebel chief. To protect Blake, Xántus made a deal with the rebel: he would recognize the chief's jurisdiction and authority if, in exchange, he would cease molesting Blake. The State Department was so displeased with this "extraordinary course" that Xántus was ordered to close the consulate, his commission was revoked, and his compensation was stopped. In spite of his financial predicament, he stayed on until the early spring of 1864 to fulfill his commitment to the Smithsonian Institution. Xántus's plight caused much concern among his fellow scientists, who considered Xántus's activities invaluable. Their solicitude is best illustrated by the anxiety of Louis Agassiz, the famed zoologist, and his efforts to help Xántus.[7]

In poor health and profoundly discouraged about his immediate prospects, Xántus once more returned to Hungary, where his two volumes of travels and his extensive gifts to the National Museum, all properly publicized, added to his lustre and made him a citizen of great distinction. He was one of the original advocates and promoters of the Zoological Garden at Budapest, and when it was founded in March

1862 he was named honorary president. In his absence the project had flagged, but it was revived on his return and in August 1866 it was officially opened with Xántus as its first director.

He was restive in his administrative post and accepted with alacrity an invitation to join the Austro-Hungarian East Asiatic Expedition in December 1868. Between 1869 and 1871 he covered Ceylon, Singapore, Siam, Indochina, Malaya, the archipelago of Indonesia, Japan, China and, after many hardships, returned with a large collection of plants and animals.

On his return he was appointed curator of the ethnographical section of the National Museum and held the post until his death on December 13, 1894, although in his last years he declined mentally.

In 1873, Olive Harper, a correspondent of the San Francisco *Daily Alta Californian*, visited Xántus and described him in her dispatch as "one of the most remarkable men of Hungary." She included the following detail in her report: "He had a particularly fine little Hindoo god, and I asked him how he had managed to get that. 'Oh!' he said 'nothing easier; I hired a man to steal it.'"

The most exhaustive study written about this gifted scientist is Henry M. Madden's *Xántus, Hungarian Naturalist in the Pioneer West* (Palo Alto, Books of the West, 1949). It is a circumstantial and critical account of the career of this remarkable explorer-adventurer, who was an extraordinary combination of rare scientific ability and quite unaffected exaggeration, even braggadocio. His vivacity and talent for dramatizing situations often led him to invent circumstances and shape happenings which had some basis of fact, but were so embroidered as to make him appear in the most favorable light. In his overweening ambition to achieve status and eminence—a pardonable objective—he was virtually obsessed by the desire to impress his family and friends with a portrait of success and accomplishment. Even after attaining a well-deserved reputation for solid scientific contributions, he was not reluctant to make up exploits of valor—not an unusual phenomenon in the unrestricted laissez-faire era of the Civil War. Such traits repeatedly appear in Madden's otherwise sympathetic account.

Yet, in spite of these character defects, one cannot help being stimulated by his inquisitive curiosity, his engaging enthusiasm, his verve and winsome eagerness, and his amiable spirit. They more than counterbalanced his failings.

In his writings he provides ample evidence of his sharp eye for intrinsic observation and his descriptive power. His incisive account of *Travels in Southern California* should fill a long-neglected void in western Americana.

Santa Barbara,
California

Theodore Schoenman

NOTES

1. Harry Harris, "Notes on the Xántus Tradition, *The Condor* 36 (Sept. 1934): 191.
2. Spencer F. Baird (1823-1887), zoologist, secretary of the Smithsonian Institution (1878); first U.S. Fish Commissioner; author of numerous scientific writings, including *North American Reptiles* (1851) and *Catalogue of North American Mammals* (1857). He instituted a system of precise ornithological description.

    George N. Lawrence (1806-1895), New York specialist in neotropical birds.

    John Cassin (1813-1869), the Philadelphia ornithologist.

    John L. LeConte (1825-1883), distinguished entomologist.

    Asa Gray (1810-1888), outstanding botanist, Fisher Professor of Natural History, Harvard University, 1842-88.

    Theodore S. Palmer, ornithologist and editor of *The Condor*.

    John Torrey, 1796-1873, eminent botanist.

    Edward Hallowell, noted collector of reptiles.

3. "The names of Audubon, Wilson, Bonaparte, Baird, Cassin and Lawrence are landmarks in the history of American ornithology, but none of them ever had the opportunity of doing any field work in California. On the other hand Heerman, Gambel, Cooper and especially Xántus were identified with active work in the field. He was one of the most energetic of the early collectors and his name is very properly borne by several species of California and Lower California birds, including Xántus' Murrelet, Xántus' Screech Owl, Xántus' Hummingbird, and Xántus' Jay." T. S. Palmer, "Five Portraits," *The Condor* 30:304.

    "Because of the extensive collections made by Xántus, Fort Tejon is the type locality for many insects, birds, other animals and plants and has become a sort of biological shrine which has been visited by scientists from the world over." Edward O. Essig, *A History of Entomology* (New York, 1931), p. 304.

    "*Eleodes veseyi.* Collected by Mr. John Xántus de Vesey; to whom I take great pleasure in dedicating the species, as a slight tribute of my appreciation of his enthusiastic labors, which have added much to our knowledge of the fauna of the Western Territories." J. L. LeConte, "Notes on the Species of Eleodes Found within the United States," *Proceedings of the Philadelphia Academy* (1858), pp. 180-88.

    "Land shells of the genus *Bulimulus* in Lower California, with descriptions of several new species. *Bulimulus (Leptobyrsus veseyianus D.)* This species is named in honor of Mr. J. Xántus de Vesey, to whom we owe much of our knowledge of the fauna of Lower California." W. H. Dall, *Proceedings U.S. National Museum* (1893), p. 645.

    "*Bothropolys xanti* W. It affords us great pleasure to dedicate this species to Mr. Xántus, through whose exhaustive collections the rich fauna, of what has

19

been a veritable "terra incognita," is being rapidly developed." H. C. Wood, "On the Chilopoda of North America," *Journal of the Philadelphia Academy* 5, ser. 2 (1862–1863): 15.

"*Amazilia xantusii* L. (Xántus hummingbird). Sent by Mr. John Xántus, whose investigations in the Ornithology of Western North America have been the means of adding many new birds to science. In compliment to him I have named it." G. N. Lawrence, "Descriptions of three new species of humming-birds," *N.Y. Lyceum Annals* 7 (1862): 109.

"The present collection was made by the indefatigable Mr. Xántus.... Small as this collection is, it contains not a few novelties, and I trust is an earnest of many more...; Mr. Xántus has already made one successful visit to the mountains within his reach, with very interesting zoological results." Asa Gray, "Enumeration of a collection of dried plants made by L. J. Xántus in Lower California," *Proceedings of the American Academy* 5 (1861): 153.

4. From a letter to Baird, dated Fort Tejon, California, November 16, 1857.

5. "... in regard to the importance of his labors ... his collections are believed to be much larger and more complete with reference to localities, than any ever before made in America during an equal space of time by a single individual." From a letter by Prof. Joseph Henry (1797–1878), secretary of the Smithsonian Institution, to Prof. A. D. Bache, superintendent of the U.S. Coast Survey, December 11, 1862.

"The general results form a fitting continuation of the labors of Mr. Xántus at Fort Tejon ... and the whole will form an extraordinary monument of the ability of a single intelligent and accomplished collector to nearly exhaust the natural history of an extensive region, under difficulties sometimes apparently almost insuperable." Smithsonian Institution, *Annual Report of the Board of Regents* (1861), p. 68.

6. Smithsonian Institution, *Annual Report of the Board of Regents* (1862), p. 41.

7.

Cambridge, Oct. 29, 1863.

My dear Baird, I am really distressed not to have a few hundred dollars at my command to relieve Xántus. I have written most entreatingly to a friend to give me some money for that object and received no answer. This failing, I have made an appeal to Prof. Henry not to allow Xántus to come back before he has accomplished his task there. Prof. Henry told me it should be his first business on returning to Washington to attend to this. I represented to him, what is emphatically true that the S.I. could not spend its money better & with greater certainty of important results. My next appropriation is not voted before the last Wednesday of this month & after that a few weeks pass by before I can cash the money & I do not even know how much I shall be allowed, otherwise I might borrow to help you. But I trust Prof. Henry will do the needful.

Very truly yours
L. Agassiz

Dedicated
to
His Excellency

AGOSTON KUBINYI

Imperial - Royal Chamberlain

and

Director of the Hungarian National Museum

as a token of his high esteem and respect

by

The Author

A few months ago a book entitled *Xántus János' Letters from North America* appeared in Laufer and Stolp's bookstore in Pest. More than half of this work, that is, the letters, were not intended for the public at large. For this reason, I have agreed to their publication only under certain conditions. These conditions were not met.

I wrote this present book specifically for publication. In order to dispel any doubt, I freely declare that I have submitted and sold this work to Laufer and Stolp who, in good faith and unaware of my conditions, bought and published my previous book. This met with my ultimate approval in granting the right to publication. I further declare that I have asked Mr. János Hunfalvy to be instrumental in my absence in supervising the publication of my travels in California.*

I take full responsibility for this work, written explicitly for publication, but I must note that it represents only a fraction of my journey

*John (János) Hunfalvy (1820–1888) geographer, was a member of the Hungarian Academy of Sciences, and founder and president of the Hungarian Geographic Society. He was educated at the University of Tübingen and University of Berlin. Imprisoned in 1849 for his part in the War of Independence of 1848, he was amnestied in 1851. He became professor of geography and statistics at the Polytechnicum of Buda, and in 1870 was named to be the first professor of geography at the University of Budapest. He was the author of many books (*Heaven and Earth* [1873], *History of* in California. The pace of life is so rapid in America that communication lags behind events. I have not yet organized the part of my voyage dealing with northern California and Oregon. I had scarcely begun to do so when I became involved in southern California with an entirely different group of people and life style.

Now, once again, I start on a new trek, and by the time these lines are in print I shall be wandering in the Cordilleras of western Mexico. I hasten to publish these segments while I may, hoping that they will be well received, if for no other reason than because, as yet, the land and peoples described here are completely unknown in Hungarian literature. I am fully conscious of the many shortcomings of this work, especially from the standpoint of style. Still it may provide the reading public with some knowledge and pleasure, and at least it accounts for the way I have spent precious time so far away from my beloved country.

Canon del Tejon, California, 5 October, 1858.   János Xántus

Geography [1878], *Geography of Africa* [1879] and others), and delegate to many international geographical congresses. He edited *African Travels* by Laszlo Magyar and *American Travel Notes* by John Xántus. Together with his brother Paul, an outstanding linguist and ethnographer, he traced the origin of Hungarian to the Finnish-Ugor language group. (Ed.)

Part I

From Los Angeles to Tejon

As readers of "Letters from North America" are aware, on June 24, 1857, I traveled south from San Francisco on the steamer *Senator* and arrived safely, passing through San Pedro, in Los Angeles, the capital of southern California, on June 28.

After the necessary preparations, on July 7 our expedition began its journey toward the Sierra Nevada.

Before I leave Los Angeles, permit me to mention some of my experiences. For the few who have had the misfortune of visiting Los Angeles, this metropolis of southern California, there is not even a semblance of a public eating place. We were forced therefore, like many others, to rent quarters. After obtaining them, naturally we had to secure our meals. For this we either had to go to a "fonda" (Spanish inn) where we would get poor quality food at prohibitive prices, or hire a cook, (thank heaven there are many of them), or start a household, which is inconvenient. Should we decide on the latter, which at any rate is the better choice, we must consider the following: either to buy the kitchen supplies ourselves, in which case the cook steals most of them, or to send the cook to the market and he steals the cash. Of the two alternatives the latter is the better, provided the cook is not overly greedy. For my part, I do not recommend firing the cook for stealing; in fact, I suggest to one who has no cook, hiring one recently dismissed for theft. A suspected thief is not nearly as dangerous as an unsuspected one.

Los Angeles has no saloons but churches galore, about one church for every 100 people. Judged by their state of crumbling decay, they must be at least 100 years old.* I can safely state that half of the city's area is occupied by churches and other religious institutions. One's first impression therefore might be that the citizens are very pious and God-fearing, but before long the very opposite becomes apparent. It seems that the clergy itself fails to tread the paths of virtue. The "quariche" (institutions for training wet nurses) of Los Angeles are famous throughout the Pacific Coast. They supply wet nurses for hundreds of miles around. Undoubtedly the reason for this is that there is a local orphanage, where a mother can leave her child without ceremony or shame, to nurse other children whose parents can pay.

The streets of Los Angeles are not elegant. The houses are low, long, and of single story, without exception. They have dark, prison-like exteriors, endless covered porches, and small windows screened by iron or wooden bars through which the female population peeps from dawn to sunset.

The markets abound with tropical fruits, poultry, game, fish, and greens, gathered mostly by Indians from the southern plains and valleys.

Those who have been in Central and South American cities will find nothing of interest in Los Angeles. But naturalists like ourselves do not regret the visit, for the flora and fauna of the vicinity are truly extraordinary. Our trips to the San Gabriel Mission, the San Bernardino Mountains, and the Santa Clara waterfall greatly enriched my collection of naturalia.

The journey to San Gabriel Mission was mentioned earlier.** Now I should like to describe briefly the waterfall mentioned above.

Señor Aguilar, the municipal magistrate invited us to join him in visiting the waterfall in the San Bernardino Mountains. The party consisted of seven men, four women, two children, four servant girls, ten peons and forty horses and mules. The ladies rode sidesaddle, while

---

*Sarcastic, not to be taken literally.
**See John Xántus, *Letters from North America* (Detroit: Wayne State University Press, 1975).

2. Carrying Goods to the Market from the Vicinity of Los Angeles

the servants rode on ordinary male style saddles. The children were carried on the backs of the peons in dossers. There were also four empty "silla" (chairs) for the ladies, in the event they became bored riding the steep trails.

Travel in a "silla" is illustrated in my drawing. It is an ordinary bamboo chair buckled to the back of the "sillero" by two straps, one across the chest and another fastened to the forehead. Of course, should the "sillero" slip and fall, the whole contraption would tumble to the ground. Obviously the passenger is at the mercy of the "sillero." It would seem it takes time and experience to become accustomed to this mode of travel; nevertheless, the ladies with whom I have traveled sat in the chairs with complete composure as if it were an everyday event. While climbing up and down on narrow trails at the edge of deep precipices, one of them slept peacefully and another read Cervantes as if she were sitting at home on a couch.

The waterfall is but a half-day's walk from the city, but the trail is so hair-raisingly terrifying that only for an exceptional reason could I be induced to ride these trails again. They are fit only for goats, and one slip of your mule might hurl you hundreds of feet into a bottomless ravine. The beautiful waterfall seemed compensation for all the sweat and terror until we realized that we had to return by the same route.

The people of Los Angeles believe the Santa Clara waterfall is higher than Niagara. They are however alone in this belief, never having seen Niagara.

Having myself seen Niagara several times, I estimate that Santa Clara is about 130 to 140 feet high, about half the height of Niagara, but sufficient to be regarded with awe by anyone. The falling mass of water turns into a rain of misty vapor before reaching the bottom; in fact, water is visible only on the top, as fog and vapor envelop the rocky floor. The roar is terrifying.

During my stay in Los Angeles I have seen many cock and bull fights as well as bear-baiting. These spectacles are an indispensable part of the Spanish heritage.

The cock and bull fights have been described by so many travelers in almost every known language that it is unnecessary to do so again, all the more as the cocks of Los Angeles fight the same way as do the Cuban or Mexican cocks. The "caballero" of Los Angeles train the wild bulls, and the bulls gore them as they do anywhere in South America—all of which was so well described by Frederick Gerstacker.

3. *The "Silla,"* unsigned

4. *Santa Clara Waterfall,* unsigned

However, the battle between a bull and a bear was a new spectacle for me. I have never read or heard of it before.

The arena is a very attractive, spacious, and expensive structure, holding easily 4,000 to 5,000 spectators on its benches. There are four main gates. Seating is in the round. The seats (loges) at the lowest elevation are some sixteen feet high while the rest are in the rear and higher up.

By five o'clock in the afternoon people were already filling the seats, and for a while a good orchestra was playing. Suddenly the music stopped and a gate opened on the north side of the arena. In stormed a wild bull foaming at the mouth, rushing to and fro, furiously, tearing at the dirt with its horns. Soon a giant of a fellow, clad in a scarlet cape and red pants, appeared facing the bull. When the bull caught sight of its guest, it rushed at him in blind fury. We all held our breath, and I for one had no doubt for a minute that Mister Red Cape would sup with Beelzebub that night. But when the bull was a pace or two in front of the man in red, he disappeared with lightning speed through a concealed door.

One can imagine how exasperated and enraged the bull was. Immediately after, we heard a loud noise and laughter on the other side of the arena. Everyone turned in that direction including the bull, and lo, the red man was now there. The bull instantly charged him, but the red man vanished once again to the unutterable chagrin of the bull. This maneuver lasted almost an hour, to the diversion and roaring laughter of the audience. Finally, to the sound of trumpets, a gate opened and a gray bear (*Ursus ferox*) of enormous size came in sight. When it noticed the bull it pricked up its ears, shook its shaggy mane, and let out a tremendous roar. Mister Bull needed but one glance at the newcomer. In seconds it encircled the bear with its horns, stabbing at its side time and time again so that everyone thought the bear would not be able to resist for long. But soon it became apparent that the bear had yielded only to surprise, and as soon as it had oriented itself and grew tired of being gored, it leaped up, shook its mane, and attacked the bull. To its misfortune and the spectators' amusement, the jump was a bit short. Just when its feet reached the ground, the bull hooked it with its horns and bowled it over. By now the bear had had enough of the fun and as its foe was about to gore it again, it dug its sharp claws into the bull's nose and held it thus. Hurt in his most sensitive part, the bull started to bellow in awesome fury; it stuck out its tongue, at which

the bear snatched with its other paw. In a few seconds, the bear had pinned the bull to the ground, and in less time than it takes to write these lines, tore out its throat and entrails.

Such is popular entertainment in southern California. During the fights the audience was in a drunken and feverish frenzy. First there was clapping and laughter, then deathly silence as the people watched every motion of the fight as if everyone's fate depended on the outcome. Not even ladies and children would miss the show. With evident delight, they enjoy this basest display of barbarism as if the finest actors and artists were performing in the arena.

This show is put on regularly, twice a week. Cockfights are a daily event. The arena is always full.

I might mention another curiosity: the many wine and lemonade vendors who ride donkeys, trotting up and down the streets. Oblong-shaped leather bags filled with wine and lemonade hang from both sides of their saddles. A box of straws (reed tubes) rests on their lap. One-half of a real is the cost of a drink. The thirsty customer sucks through a straw as much as he can in one draft. When he stops swallowing he has finished his drink. If he wants more he has to pay again.

July 7. Our saddles, baggage, and wagons have been ready since yesterday. This morning we packed and started on our way. To spare our mules an excessive burden, so that they would not reach the Sierra Nevada exhausted but in full strength, I hired wagons and loaded the baggage on them.

Our caravan is composed of the strangest individuals. California is matchless in this respect. I do not believe that there is a corner anywhere on earth (including even Australia) where as many adventurers of all nationalities gather, as they do in this Eldorado. Had I spent years in California in an attempt to assemble the most remarkable bunch of scoundrels, I could not have done better than with the members of this group. They are all volunteers and at the time, residents of Los Angeles.

Of the eight wagon drivers, one is a Norwegian counterfeiter, another an escaped galley slave from Naples, the third a French counterfeiter, the fourth a rowdy from New Orleans, the fifth a Prussian deserter, the sixth an escaped deportee from Australia, the seventh a Malayan, and the eighth from the Sandwich Islands.

Our cook is a Portuguese sailor and a Negro is in charge of the provisions. Among our muleteers were two Americans, one Dane, one

5. *Wine and Lemonade Vendor, Los Angeles*, unsigned

Mexican, one Indian, one Chilean, two Peruvians and two Chinese. Finally, the scientific members consist of two Englishmen, a Scot, a Frenchman, two Americans, a German and my modest self, representing Hungary and leading the expedition.

But all these are surpassed by Antonio, the *carrièro principale*, or chief muleteer and wagon driver. Antonio, because of his high position and even greater qualifications, is called Don Antonio by all. He was born in Madagascar. In his early youth he landed in Mexico and has lived for the last twenty years in California. He participated in various capacities in many campaigns of the republic and in countless expeditions against the Arapahoe and Apache Indians. He is the most renowned bear and mustang hunter in all of southern California.

For years he was responsible for crushing every robber band in the area. In consequence, Don Antonio became an important personage, so that when I asked the magistrate to recommend a *carrièro principale* who could lead us through the snowcapped Sierra Nevada, he was greatly astonished and pitied me for not knowing Don Antonio. Naturally, upon such high recommendation, I hired him at once and according to custom, entrusted him to use his judgment in the recruitment of our personnel. I have already mentioned the kind of company mustered by Señor Antonio.

It would sound comical to anyone who could overhear his way of communicating with our men. Even in this respect Don Antonio tops us all. He can talk with anyone, understands everyone, and makes himself understood by all. Having often had similar experiences, he invented for his own convenience a special language which is a colorful mixture of all the known and unknown tongues of the world, spiced with the most fanciful swear words. These last he uses when someone does not understand him, or, according to him, does not want to. He is convinced that his curses are not only understood by all but induce instant obedience to his orders.

Antonio is on horseback from dawn to dusk. From horseback he supervised the loadings of all the supplies and, to steel himself for this important task, he arrayed on the pommel of his saddle a half-dozen bull horns. The reader need not be alarmed. The horns contained neither gunpowder nor anything lethal, but only "chica," a spirit made of grapes, of which he takes a snort every five minutes.

Antonio's appearance is as unusual as his personality. His

headgear is a bright red snood resembling a nightcap which is held down by an inimitably braided Sonora cane hat, tied to his chin against the wind. I have not been able as yet to peek at his undergarments, as his middle is covered with a red poncho and his legs with long buffalo-hide leggins. From his heels, cruel-looking spurs protrude. They are four inches in diameter with long, sharp, pointed spikes, not, as he remarked, for his own but the horse's benefit.

Around nine o'clock we saddled our horses and started the caravan, although by then, four of our men were in the "calaboose" for drunkenness, brawling, and shooting. The chief of police assured us that they would be freed as soon as they sobered up. Antonio pledged his honor that by latest next morning they would be in our camp.

The southeastern part of the city, from where we started, is surrounded for many miles by sandy hillocks. Soon our train moved through them, and the city with its lush vegetation and pleasant landscape faded from our view. We advanced through a seemingly endless forest of cacti. I say "forest" advisedly, because these cacti often reach the height of twenty five to thirty feet and the diameter of the trunk as much as three feet (*Cactus yucca*). But outside of the cacti which decorate the shifting sand, there is hardly any other vegetation.

Of the animal world we saw only two species of rabbits, these however in abundance (*Lepus callotis* and *Lepus trowbrigii*). They were so tame that they could be shot from the roadside with pistols. Towards evening we reached the Carvingo Mountains* where we proceeded among narrow defiles until we came upon a lovely spring where we set up camp.

In the morning our four wagoneers arrived, now freed from jail. *July 8.* Soon after starting out, we reached the top of the mountain range and descended along the eastern slope. Around noon we rested at Carvingo Rancho. A "rancho" is somewhat like an inn or camp on our own Hungarian plain.

In southern California the dry season lasts from March to November, during which time not even a drop of rain falls. For this reason people settle near a river or brook or spring, where cattle can graze and drink and the settler can raise a crop. But intensive agriculture is difficult in such environment because there is sufficient

---

*Called the San Gabriel Mountains today.

moisture only at the water's edge and the farmer cannot plow the soil for miles alongside the water; consequently, even though he is settled near the water, he still must water his field daily.

Irrigation is done in the same way as in Italy or on the Hungarian plain where rice is planted. The field is crisscrossed with furrows filled with water. Naturally, such laborious cultivation is possible only on a small scale, a maximum of four to five acres. Sufficient food for only the household can be produced and the important industry is cattle, horse, and sheep raising. In this respect the ranch resembles the farms of our own plains.

Carvingo Rancho is such a place. Don José Madriguez, the owner, claims he does not know how many horses he owns, but estimates them to number about 15,000. Señor Madriguez received us most cordially, showed us around his estate and then treated us to a good dinner. Although his father and grandfather lived and died here, he had not much to show for it in the way of improvements. Here and there a few grapevines and one or two orange and olive trees comprised his entire plantation.

His house is very much   n old dilapidated "curia" (manor house) from the era of Maria Theres,. It is built of adobe clay with a columned veranda in front, and a reed roof. If I were to picture birch and chestnut trees instead of palms and cacti around the house, I could easily believe us to be in the Hungarian countryside.

The Carvingo Desert or Llano Carvingo* starts here. While not too extensive in area, it is extremely exhausting to man or beast, for it consists entirely of shifting sand dunes. Moreover, our journey took place in July when the sun mercilessly beats down upon the unfortunate and misguided traveler. I dared not continue in the afternoon in such heat. We let the cattle graze and water at sundown and left only after midnight.

July 9. By sunrise we had traversed half the desert with little trouble, for the nights are cool. This desert, although monotonous, is not without interest. I never saw so many lizards and rattlesnakes in one place. In fact I had to send four men with whips in advance to clear our road so we might proceed. It seemed that whole families of reptiles were stretched out on the road to enjoy the warmth of the rising sun. Most of these snakes are of a species found in Texas, but I also found many that are substantially different from those in the eastern and southern states.

The head and the back of this snake are covered with small, overlapping scales resembling those of a fish, whereas the eastern and southern rattlers are overlaid with larger plates, entirely different from the small scales covering the rest of the body (*Crotalus atrox*. Baird and Girard, *Crotalus lucifer* B. and G.).

The *Crotalus lucifer* is easily recognizable, and it is just as well, for it is the most aggressive and venomous of the species. The color is shiny black with tiny, pale yellow intersecting squares stretching the length of the body. The fully-grown specimen is five feet long. When it reaches this stage it no longer grows in length but in bulk. I killed an exceptionally fat specimen. Its length was 4 feet 10 inches, the neck 4¼ inches and the waist 10½ inches thick. I found two undigested hamsters, hair and skin intact, in its stomach, which accounted for the unusual bulk.

On this same desert for the first time I came across the famous Mexican pheasant, or the roadrunner as the Spanish call it (*Correo del camino, Geococcyx mexicanus* Gambel). This is truly a most unusual bird if what is attributed to it is true: it never flies, trusting its feet more than its wings; it runs from its enemies. Mexicans often chase it on horseback for miles into barren fields, the more easily to get at it with their whips. Even so, they find places to hide and often escape.

I should have liked to race the pheasants myself, but among the profusion of cacti it was out of the question. I got off my horse and walked for miles ahead of the column, my rifle on the ready, but no luck. Here and there one crossed my path, vanishing with lightning speed like a phantom. Since then, I was fortunate to acquire two specimens, male and female. The latter I shot myself on the Calavese plain, the other one I got from an Indian. The bird is much smaller than the common Hungarian pheasant, but the tail is at least twice as long. The back is dark brown with golden green flecks. The wings are of the same color with three diagonal yellow lines. The tail is grey, dotted with red spots. The underfeathers are of chamois color or pale orange yellow. The male has an ultramarine crest on its head, resembling that of a peacock, which he is able to move in all directions. Both specimens are in perfect condition and I shall forward them to the Hungarian National Museum with the next collection.

The very unusual animal life we found on our route kept us in perpetual excitement, so that the time went by so fast that we almost regretted when around noon we reached a hard clay road, where, as if by magic, there was a complete change of the flora. Dwarf oleanders, orange and olive trees mixed with some pine and shrub oaks took the place of the cacti. These latter, with their pale coloring, were a pleasing contrast to the virulent sharp green of the orange and olive trees.

Step by step the vegetation grew more lush, until it became a veritable forest where we encountered numerous birds of brilliant plumage, particularly woodpeckers, jays, and magpies. (Among others were: *Pica nuttalli* and *Pica bullockii; Garrulus ultramarinus, Californianus* and *Stelleri; Pica formicivorus, torquatus, ruber* and *Picus imperialis sat.* This last one is the largest and rarest woodpecker known. From back to tail it measures 27 inches. Its color is an iridescent blue and green intermixed with black; the wings are snow white and the head is yellow with a 3-inch scarlet red crest.)*

Soon we were out of the forest and a beautiful meadow unfolded, covered with flowers. Less than two miles before us on the mountainside was San Fernando, where we arrived in short order and set up camp.

The area called South California extends from a northern latitude of 32° as far as 36°, that is from the Gulf of California all the way to the Tulare Desert. It is 240 miles in width and about 450 miles in length, west to east. Almost the entire region is crisscrossed by barren, jagged mountains, enclosing numerous sandy deserts, and adorned by nothing but various species of giant cacti.

Wherever water is found however, everything is transformed by the hot climate, as if by magic, into astonishing fertility. In countless valleys the traveler can admire the great beauty of the tropical flora. Sugarcane and indigo grow here in perfection found nowhere else in North America. Olive and fig trees, orange, lemon, and pomegranate, and many other plants native to the lush southern climate, as well as grapevines which produce excellent wine, luxuriate in the countryside. There are many salt lakes and salt plains at the foot of the Sierra Nevada. Gold and silver are mined in many places, and on the shores of the Purple Sea (Gulf of California) large quantities of genuine pearl, coral, and sponge are to be found.

*Yellow-billed magpie, Steller's jay, California crow, etc.

South California was colonized by the Jesuits in 1697. As far as the natives were concerned, they were benevolent colonizers (if only in this case), for they occupied the land without bloodshed or coercion, solely by the means of their religious influence. There were about 50,000 Indians here at that time. The Jesuits signed a treaty and established friendly relations with them, and utilizing their good will, completely changed their lives within a very short period of time.

They built fourteen missions, which served as gathering points for the local Indians where, sheeplike, they unquestionably entrusted body and soul to the saintly fathers. As every writer of the period agrees, one could hardly find more humble and obedient believers than these savages.

The rapidly growing influence and power of the Jesuits in the New World ultimately created jealousy in the Spanish government, resulting in their banishment from the colonies in 1767. The leader of the military expedition (Portola) arrived with a fleet of war ships in California. He came to carry out the orders of the government and to occupy the land in the name of His Most Catholic Majesty. He expected to find enormous amounts of treasures in the missions, defended by whole legions of Jesuits and thousands upon thousands of Indians. Hardly had he stepped ashore with his troops when he was humbly approached by the Jesuits (a few silver-haired ancients), followed by crying and wailing, unarmed Indians. The general (so claimed an eyewitness) was so touched by this unexpected spectacle that he shed tears, but his orders had to be carried out. The Jesuits were made to embark and were immediately sent off amidst the lamentations of thousands of Indians who for days watched the ships in great distress.

Most of the Indians returned shortly to the mountain wilderness, their ancestral habitat, and reverted gradually to the savagery of their forefathers a century before. Later, the government sent out a few Dominicans, but they exercised little influence. Ultimately the Franciscans took over the missions which as of today they still hold, although only two of them, San Gabriel and San Fernando, still flourish. The others decayed and are mostly in ruins.

It is noteworthy that while at present the land belongs to the United States, where unabridged religious freedom prevails, the Jesuits are not reoccupying their mission houses. No one is preventing them from doing so and they could do much to help improve the lot of

39

the poor Indians. It is also true, however, that since California is part of the United States, everyone enjoys equal rights. There is no more master and serf. Everyone works for money and not gratis, and this principle is as well understood by the half-civilized Indian as by any "completely civilized" horse-and-carriage driver in New York.

San Fernando provides a good example of the former power and affluence of the Jesuits. The cloister and church are truly magnificent buildings. The former was the residence at one time of the Jesuit abbot. It stands on one of the most westerly spurs of the Sierra Nevada, on the edge of an indescribably beautiful and rich valley. The view is extraordinary. On the distant horizon to the south glitters the Purple Sea; to the west, the Carvingo desert with the similarly named mountain range in the background; to the northeast rise the sugarloaf-shaped peaks of the Sierra Nevada, covered with eternal snow. The dark blue skies, the prodigious variety of flora, and the delightful bird life conjure up an enchanted landscape which can be gazed at with wonder, but cannot be described.

The church and cloister are built of carved stone. The latter has one story. The church is an extensive structure with two steeples, the walls of which are six feet thick and covered with a stone vault three feet in diameter. The cloister is partly in ruins. Only two Dominican friars live there. The flooring is rotting, the winds howl through the windows and cacti grow on the sills.

About fifteen square leagues belong to the mission and 1,600 Indians are cared for, most of whom live in small, whitewashed, adobe buildings scattered around the mission. The institution is quite successful in the promotion of Indian welfare, for many tanners, bootmakers, weavers, smiths, stonemasons and other craftsmen are trained. A special group takes care of the agriculture, and another one is occupied with the care of thousands of horses, mules, sheep, and cattle. The women spin, weave, sew, and in general do the chores of women in normal civilized life. They have 1,500 acres of land under cultivation in two separately fenced areas. One of these is planted solely with grapes, with the exception of forty acres, where greens and other garden vegetables are grown. The other garden is reserved for a fruit orchard. Peaches, walnuts, oranges, figs, lemons, pineapples and pomegranates are planted on its 600 acres, which are bordered on both sides with olive trees. The crop of these trees provides a good part of the mission's income.

6. *San Fernando, South California*, original drawing by John Xántus, 1858; print by Haske & Co., Pest, 1859

Besides the above, much barley is raised, and although the shade of the trees delays the maturation of the seed, the land still yields three crops a year. The autumn planting is completely ripe by early April, the second planting by July, and the third one by the end of October. All this clearly proves that cereal grains could be raised here, if only in limited quantities. But there is no marketplace where the crop might be sold. That is why no one has attempted it.

The mission's revenue is under the sole control of the priests, but it must be admitted that the flock under their care suffer no want and in many respects enjoy comforts.

Horses and cattle are also a source of substantial income, even though they are unbelievably cheap. The horses are small and not of the best bloodline, but the mules are really good. Today I bought a horse for three dollars and two mules for fifteen dollars. I had my pick from a stud of 5,000 animals.

July 10. As so often happens on expeditions of this kind, we noticed only yesterday the many small things that need correction: things went wrong with the saddles or tools, or the baggage came apart, or many horses needed treatment of one sort or another. In general there was hardly anything that did not need fixing, so we devoted yesterday and today to attending to everything before moving into the mountains.

Every member of the company took advantage of the two-day holiday to roam over the mission, looking into every nook and cranny. We were received with great cordiality and, as is the custom in every mission, the priests are very hospitable to everyone, regardless of rank or religion—affirming the Christian principle.

The reverend fathers gave the company permission to slaughter as many sheep and cattle as they needed for food, the sole condition being that the hides must be turned in. The mission also arranged a horse race and a bullfight in our honor and these spectacles were much enjoyed by the men. But above all, they liked the Californians' riding skill. We can no longer call them Indians for they are all civilized now; they speak, read, and write Spanish; they drink and gamble, and so on.*

As horses are plentiful and inexpensive, naturally everyone seems to be a natural born caballero or horseman. Indeed, the local

---

*Xántus is being sarcastic.

Indians, Mexicans and half-breeds spend most of their lives in the saddle. Consequently, they are all daring riders whose expert and hazardous maneuvers on untamed and wild colts and horses is worthy of admiration, and we were much impressed even though we have seen the prairie Commanche.

The California horseman in many respects resembles the Andalusian knights of De Vega or Cervantes. He wears a wide-brimmed peaked hat, a silver-braided dolman, trousers slit at the side from the knee down, revealing red socks underneath, and he sits on a saddle decorated with peacock feathers. The jackboot is armed with huge spurs which are fastened to the heels with heavy chains—the clinking sound can be heard a half mile away. Ordinarily he carries on the pommel a pistol with a long barrel, trimmed with fox or squirrel tail, and a sharp dagger; sitting thus in the saddle, he no doubt believes he is nothing less than "California's pride and the scourge of the terrified universe."

The California caballero seldom rides without a lasso, which is a long rope rolled with a loop on one end, and which he uses with extraordinary skill. In my childhood I had heard of the custom in Transylvania and Bukovina of catching horses with a loop, but I have never seen anything like it in Europe. It seems certain that at present this weapon is used only in Spanish America, although according to Prescott, the famous historian, it is of Asian origin. According to him the Persians employed it long ago, when 8,000 soldiers armed with it participated in Xerxes' campaigns. The Spanish Americans use the lasso for various purposes, among them to gather wood. The California caballero never dismounts when he gathers wood; he stays on his horse and loops the lasso around a tree trunk or log. He fastens the end of the lasso to the saddle and drags home the firewood. Wild cattle and wild horses are captured in the same fashion.

Undoubtedly, one of the more important functions of the lasso is to catch bears, which provides the local populace with much—if barbaric—amusement. Bears are caught in the following manner: normally three to four caballeros ride into a forest where bears are known to be, place the carcass of a cow or calf in a clearing, and then hide nearby. They don't have to wait long, for the bears soon appear, following the scent of an unexpected meal. As soon as a bear is in a position that suits the purpose of the caballero, he rushes forth from his hiding place and lassoes it. Having accomplished this, he gallops ahead, drag-

43

ging the bear after him until it is totally exhausted. Then he ties up the weary animal and triumphantly takes it into the arena. By this time the animal is usually in a great fury and the caballero often sprays it with cold water to cool its temper. One can well imagine how dangerous it would be for both horse and rider if the bear should break loose while in such paroxysm of rage. This is the way they ordinarily catch them for bear fights.

During our stay in San Fernando, I visited the various shops to see for myself the progress of the natives. While they can make heavy blankets, all kinds of carpets and capes of extraordinary beauty, and manufacture all their agricultural tools from plows to kitchen knives themselves, still the equipment of the shops is quite primitive. Needless to say, this is not the Indians' fault.

I am enclosing a drawing of the smithy and of one of the weaving rooms, from which it should be clear how much arduous labor is required of these poor people to produce their necessities.

July 11. We sent our wagons ahead yesterday afternoon and this morning our caravan continued its journey. Having no heavy burden, I did not follow the customary wagon trail at the foot of the mountains, but choosing a shorter mule track, headed straight up into the mountains. Because of this, after a few hours' ride, we found ourselves on the topmost ridge of the mountain spur. From there, for the first time I saw the snowcapped Sierra Nevada range in its full grandeur, as I have only seen it before in my dreams. To the north, east, and southeast as far as the eye can see, huge mountains with snowcovered peaks seem to reach into the sky, which toward the north rise even higher until they dissolve in a veil of fog. To the southwest, the eye wanders over a seemingly endless wilderness and on the distant horizon we see what appears to be a vapor-covered snow desert, although we know well enough that it is the Carvingo Desert and the Purple Sea (Gulf of California).

Anyone who is acquainted with my humble self can well imagine with what feeling of excitement and glowing state of mind I approached this wildly romantic world, which if fate so wills it, will be the scene of my adventures in the next few years.

Late in the afternoon we arrived at Fort Reid, which is in the Sierra Nevadas and which serves partly as a shelter for travelers in case of a storm, and partly as a defense post against hostile Indian tribes. The fort is built of wood, 3,500 feet above sea level and is garrisoned by twenty mounted hunters under the command of a lieutenant.

Our wagons were already waiting for us at Fort Reid. I paid them off and discharged them, for this is the end of the wagon trail. From tomorrow on we shall travel on a footpath and in a few days we shall be climbing mountains.

July 12. We started after midnight and our path soon led us to a branch of the San Francisquita River, rushing down from the snowy mountains. Following its capricious turns upward, we crossed it many times when the path zigzagged from one shore to the other under the vertical ridges. The dense vegetation soon disappeared and a variety of pine and thorny underbrush—similar to the blackthorn in Hungary—took its place. In many spots the path led us through miles of thorns and, because of the narrowness of the path and the density of the brush, not only our trousers but our own skin started to rub off against our knees by noontime.

Also around noon the first patches of snow appeared around the source of the creek. From there the path led up and down a narrow ridge to the rim of a gaping chasm, the edge of which we followed upward. Soon the trail became like a narrow ribbon winding its way amidst the rocks. To the left, vertical basalt and granite cliffs were rising to a height of several hundred feet, while to the right, a terrifying precipice was gaping, the walls of which descended almost perpendicularly, and from the depths of the helter-skelter heaps of rock, the dull murmur of the creek could be heard. At some places the trail narrowed so much that our packs and often our knees scraped the cliff walls, and one misstep could have meant an inevitable plunge into the depth. Although many accidents happen every year and countless number of travelers and mules find their graves in these giant abysses, those who are used to this kind of travel have no great fear of mishaps; and truly, if the mule is surefooted and the rider prudent and levelheaded, the chances of accidents, although they are not to be excluded, are slim. It is difficult to imagine to what extent the mule senses that its surefootedness in such places means its very life. If the trail is good and wide enough, the mule progresses rapidly; if it is poor and narrow it calculates its steps so carefully and so close to the cliff wall, that one marvels at its unerring instinct. In some places, crevices several feet wide intersect the trail, while at others it is covered with snow and ice. Reaching such places, the mule invariably stops and waits for his master to dismount or to remove its load. The first time we reached such a spot, the trail was covered with snow for fifteen feet and my mule stopped. I did not know how to dismount. To the right I would have

45

7. *Indian Smithy* (San Fernando, South California), original drawing by John
Xántus, 1858; print by Haske & Co., Pest, 1859

8. *Indian Weaving Room* (San Fernando, South California); original drawing by John Xántus, 1858; print by Haske & Company, Pest, 1859

stepped into the gaping chasm, to the left my knee was scraping the cliff wall. I did not figure on this eventuality ahead of time and so I did not notice how Don Antonio—who rode ahead of me—dismounted. Finally on the advice of the Peruvian riding right behind me, I slid onto the buttock of the mule and slowly lowered myself behind it. How well the poor animal sensed that both our lives depended on this maneuver is indicated by the fact that during the entire operation of dismounting, it leaned its body to the left against the wall and planted its feet solidly against the rim. I had hardly slid off its back, when it slowly started off, feeling with its hooves the spots on which to tread. I followed in its traces and when the trail widened, it stopped and I remounted.

Antonio issued many instructions to the company and we found them, almost without exception, to be useful and practical. Among other things, he suggested riding without stirrups and leaning the upper body towards the cliff walls whenever the trail narrowed or was slippery. Riding in this manner in such hazardous places has an advantage: should the animal slip and plunge into the depths, the rider has a slight chance of saving himself. Not having his foot in the stirrup and sitting in an angled position, he would necessarily fall toward the wall and grasp hold of something—provided he does not lose his presence of mind—and even more important, he would have something to hold on to.

On our way we passed by two shelters which are usually erected in places where there is sufficient room for travelers and their animals, and where wood and water is accessible. But our caravan was large and we could not camp comfortably in these places, and so we decided to continue to the so-called "plaza," which we reached safely at five in the afternoon, after sixteen hours of uninterrupted and harrowing scramble. The "plaza" is a wide open space extending over about five acres on which there are a number of log cabins for the use of any traveler, and although they are furnished only with two fireplaces, two tables and a few benches, even this offers considerable comfort in a place like this.

To gather firewood was quite difficult, the many travelers on this route cleared away every bush over a wide area. Six men were sent out for this purpose and they returned late at night with only enough firewood to prepare tea. After caring for, as best we could, and securing the animals for the night, everyone of us lay down wrapped in our blankets.

9. *California Mountain Sheep,* unsigned

The "plaza" is at an elevation of 11,400 feet* and this sudden rise in a tropical climate greatly affects the nervous system. Most everyone suffers from headaches, many complain of stomach cramps, and very few are able to sleep the night through. All of us were cold. At eight o'clock in the evening the thermometer stood at 36° (Fahrenheit) whereas yesterday at the same time it was 87° at Fort Reid.

This being Sunday, I was beseeched all day long by our men, especially the Peruvians, to say mass or at least preach a sermon as soon as we reach camp. In spite of my protestation that not being a priest I know nothing of such things, I could not dissuade them and finally had to promise that if they could find a prayer book, I would read them the Sunday prayers and sing a litany in which they could join me. This was received with great joy, but when we reached camp, the ones who wanted the mass most were the ones who shivered the most, so they forgot about the mass and the sermon, rolled themselves up in their blankets, and were soon snoring away.

Several times in the afternoon we saw large herds of mountain goats and sheep. The former were quite wild (*Aplocerus montanus* Richardson) and upon approach, became frightened and ran from us, leaping onto the jagged rocks. The latter, however, just stared at us and did not seem to be afraid. At times they merely grazed and stared at us from a shooting distance. Many naturalists thought and still think that the American mountain sheep (*Ovis montana* Cuvier) is identical with the *Kamchatkan argali*. This however is a great error, for aside from the major differences in the anatomical structure of the species, as demonstrated by Professor Baird's latest work (*Catalogue of North American Mammals*, Washington, 1857), the external structure of the animals clearly show the difference between the two species. Although I have never seen a *Kamchatkan argali*, I happen to possess a good drawing of it (Pallas, *Naturgeschichte merkwürdiger Thiere*, vol. XI tab. I et II)** and it takes only one glance to see that the two animals are altogether different. Although many naturalists try to prove that not only the marten, the beaver, and the red bear (*Mustela americana* Turton, *Castor canadiensis* Kuhl, *Ursus cinnamoneus* Audubon) but also the mountain sheep are identical in Asia and America, I am not inclined to credit these assertions and am thoroughly convinced that

---

*This figure is questionable and is possibly a misprint in the original copy.
**Pallas, *Natural History of Unusual Animals*, a German encyclopedia of zoology.

not a single American mammal is identical with its Asian counterpart. Believing this, I would unhesitatingly state that the habitat of the mountain sheep is restricted to the Rocky Mountains and the Sierra Nevadas, except for the few specimens which may be seen periodically in northern Mexico.[1] The female is a small animal with short, backward curving goatlike horns; its color is snow-white in the winter and light gray in the summer. The ram, however, is an imposing looking fellow. Its color is dark brown, the body is covered with coarse, thick hair. The horns curve downward behind the ears and forward in a semicircle and they are so huge that some weigh as much as sixty pounds and the circumference at the base is not less than two-and-a-half feet. A fully developed specimen weighs as much as 400 pounds.

July 13. Starting early in the morning we continued our arduous journey. Today the trail was hazardous only in spots but was by no means easy. Mostly it led through wide, barren slabs of rock, here and there among snowdrifts which slid off the higher peaks, and in general it was steeper than yesterday. In a few places we had to tie up the packs with long ropes and, with the help of several mules, pull them up. At last around noon we reached the top of the snowy ridge without a mishap and pitched camp on a plateau.

As far as the eye can see the entire region is an indescribable "topsy-turvy world." Wherever we looked, the same terrifying, craggy, unclimbable peaks faced us, and the geological formation seems to make one believe that at one time these peaks constituted the surface of the earth and the basins, plains, and plateaus are the results of sinking and submersion.

At an elevation of over 13,000 feet,* quite naturally we observed great changes in the atmosphere. Most of our men complained of cramps, many had their tongues and lips ulcerated, and all of us suffered from headaches.

Partly to make barometric observations and partly to gain a more perspective view of the area, I decided to climb one of the tall peaks and, with a few companions, quickly jumped into saddle. One of the slopes offered the possibility of reaching the snow banks on muleback without difficulty and we were not disappointed in this, for the entire slope consisted of crumbling stone and gravel which we easily climbed. But when we reached the top, we found ourselves, to our amazement,

---

*Possible misprint in original text.

at the rim of a precipice and the snow banks, rising straight across from us, covered an even higher peak. Leaving our mules in the care of one of our men, we descended the slope and climbed up on the other side and continued wearily until we reached the top. We almost despaired at the thought of finding ourselves at the edge of yet another abyss and opposite another peak even higher than the one we climbed.

At first I thought that these summits were isolated and disconnected mountains, but now it began to dawn on me that they are part of a chain on top of a mountain range, separated from one another by lengthy crevasses. To solve this problem I therefore felt duty bound to continue the climb until a sufficiently wide vista opened up to make fairly accurate geographical observations.

As night was fast approaching I sent out one of my friends for some blankets and instructed him to have the mules returned to our base camp and to have the expedition continue at dawn towards the Mojave River, where they were to wait for us. They were to leave two men and six mules and sufficient food behind for us at the present camp.

By the time our friend returned we had already climbed the next peak, and were sitting comfortably—considering the circumstances—in a deep crevasse smoking our pipes. For many years now it has become my habit to carry tobacco with me even when I go for a short walk. This habit now came in handy. We had plenty of matches and having nothing to light but tobacco, we amused and warmed ourselves by just striking them. Huddled together like animals we were soon in the arms of Morpheus and slept soundly until the morning.

July 14. We continued climbing and soon were in the very womb of these fearsome mountains. Our only good fortune was that sheep and goats preceded us and we could follow their footsteps, although these trails led us sometimes to such hair-raising obstacles that, being unable to advance, we had to retrace our path with great difficulty and start in a new direction. But the further we struggled the higher the dark and vertical bastions loomed. We were about to abandon our plan in despair when we sighted a breach which seemed to lead to the tallest peak and appeared to be climbable. Following the impulse, we started the climb at once and after much effort reached the top, but once again found ourselves among still higher towering rocks. Having gotten this far, we picked out the highest cliff and, after a short rest, started climbing again. Soon we realized what an immense undertaking this was, but a man's pride and desire to dominate is never greater and more stubborn than when climbing a mountain, and so retreat was out of the question. We had long ago left behind our blankets as cumbersome hindrances, and now had shed our jackets too. Soaked with perspiration, we advanced on all fours, stuffing fistfuls of snow into our burning throats every once in a while.

At last, after much perseverance, we reached the top, where a panorama of such magnitude unfolded before our eyes that we were filled with wonder and awe. We were standing on that dividing ridge which the Indians of south California call "the crest of the world" and from where—we can state this with certainty—the view slants toward the two main oceans of the world. The viewer is literally bewildered by the immensity and variety of the landscape. Beneath us the Sierra Nevadas seemed to reveal all their secrets: deep, brooding valleys, mirror-smooth lakes, ghastly fractures, hair-raising mountain passes, frightening obstacles, and foaming creeks. We stood engrossed and stared wild-eyed at the vastness of the panorama, which seemed to be limited only by the sinking horizon. Like the sea at summer, the skyline drifted into a veil of fog. Wherever we looked we saw limitless plains shimmering in the sun, interlaced with rivers resembling silver ribbons which, flowing in their melancholy way, carried the elements to the great oceans of the world. To the north we saw snowy peaks, the outlines of which became fainter and fainter as the clouds enveloped them in the distance.

At last we too almost began to believe the legendary myth of the Mojave Indians, according to which, this place is where the fallen warrior first sees the world of the spirit and the happy land where wildlife is inexhaustible and the hunter's bliss is limitless.

For a long time we stood silent on the mountaintop, immersed in our emotions and flights of fancy, then we took a deep breath and came down to earth and to our task which was to make accurate observations of the region.

The ridge on which we stood completely dominates the entire southwestern wing of the Sierra Nevadas, and although it is geographically a side branch only, it is still in itself an immense mountain range with numerous branching spurs and countless valleys. Most of these latter embrace lakes and are entwined with rushing creeks and springs which can be considered the sources of many great rivers flowing into the Pacific Ocean. To the southeast we saw the twisting, turning

10. *The Summit of the Sierra Nevada*, original drawing by John Xántus, July 13, 1858; print by Haske & Co., Pest, 1859

Mojave River until in the far distance it disappears without a trace in the spongy lava desert. To the east, the western branches of the Colorado River are visible until they snake into the San Francisco Mountains, where they disappear from view. To the west, almost beneath our feet, is the Santa Clara River which begins its course as a mountain stream hardly worthy of notice, dashing boldly down the mountains until at last it reaches respectable proportions and flows into the Pacific Ocean.

The sun is particularly bright, the weather tranquil and the atmosphere is so clear that one can see to an amazing distance.

At last the breeze, the snow, and the altitude chilled us to the bone and so immediately after making our barometric and meteorological observations, we began our descent. We were glad to reach the place where we left our jackets, which we put on at once, buttoning them to the chin. In a few hours we found our blankets too, which we used to good advantage as capes, and although we had planned to spend the night in the same "hotel" as the night before, by the time we stumbled there we were so cold and hungry that we decided to continue to the base camp in spite of the lateness of the hour.

It was well past midnight by the time we got there and an unexpected surprise and pleasure awaited us—a crackling fire. Our men had roamed all over to gather pine branches for firewood. I do not know whether for their own comfort or in our honor, but no matter, regardless of motives, we were grateful for it.

July 15. Our small group descended the northeastern slope without difficulty and late in the evening joined the caravan, which since yesterday was waiting for us on the bank of the Mojave River. I had hardly hoped to accomplish this very difficult part of our journey without any mishap, but we did so without any problems, which is a rare occurrence considering the size of the expedition and the desolate mountainous wilderness where all life seems to be absent.

However, in spite of the barren and frightfully grim aspect of the region with its almost unclimbable rock cliffs, it still has some human habitation. While one of the men awaiting us with the mules went hunting, he came across the track of a solitary human in the snowdrifts. From sheer curiosity he followed the tracks and when he reached the top of the ridge, to his great astonishment he saw three Indians quite close by. The Indians saw him at the same time and started to run. Our man shouted for them to stop and, convinced that there is no one on earth who does not understand his language, he thought that they did not hear him, so following the American custom he fired his rifle to make them hear and stop. At this, the savages ran even faster and soon disappeared. This man related the story when we reached camp and it immediately occurred to me that these savages may perhaps belong to those Indian nations which Hernandez described a century ago as living alone or in small groups on top of these mountains or in places which are almost inaccessible. Presumably, they speak the Mojave language, which would indicate that they are a branch of the Mojave tribe, although their present customs and life style are entirely different. As one can imagine, they are all miserably poor, have no animals, and lack all articles of comfort which they could acquire through contact with the white man. Their weapons are the bow and arrow; the arrow tip is a sharply chiselled pointed stone with which they hunt mountain goats, sheep, wolves, the animals which supply most of their food and clothing.

Hunters often find their tracks among the highest peaks and see the smoke of their fires coiling among the rocks, which provides many a learned traveler with the unexpected pleasure of seeing "a dormant volcano in the Sierra Nevada." (Dr. Moritz Wagner and Karl Scherzer, *Reisen in Nordamerika in den Jahren 1852 und 1853* [Leipzig, 1854], 3 vols. Written in collaboration with the Austrian geographer, Karl Scherzer.)[2] It is seldom that one meets these Indians and even more rare to persuade them to enter into conversation. Their pitiful poverty is no temptation to other, rapacious Indian tribes, and since they hurt no one, no one pursues them. If, however, the Mojave or Tejon Indians capture one, they invariably scalp him if for no other reason than to be able to dance the "scalp dance," the favorite entertainment of all North American Indians.

This morning as we were descending the mountains, I lagged behind a little and had the unexpected good fortune of seeing these savages close by. As I stepped from a gully onto the trail, I noticed three of them hardly more than a couple of steps in front of—or rather above—me. They were hiding behind an obione* bush watching with great curiosity every move I made. Two of them stood right under the bush, pressed close together, while the third was kneeling somewhat behind them. All three of them had quivers, bows and arrows, and their clothing consisted of a few pieces of wolf skin. Wishing to see them eye to eye, I placed a couple of silver dollars in my hands and, showing it to them, I accosted them. But much to my regret they immediately ran off.

Probably they were the same three our men saw the day before.

July 16. Yesterday as we rejoined the expedition, we found a Mojave chief there with his hunters. He was extremely friendly and talkative and entertained the company all day long. His name is Yumusruy-Ekahat-Hum, but I will spare the reader and mention him by name only when absolutely necessary. I had hardly arrived in the camp, when I had to promise him that tomorrow (that is today) I shall stop over at one of the larger villages of his tribe. He sent off messengers at once, to have his people make appropriate preparations for our reception.

Traveling upriver in a northeasterly direction, the land appeared to be fertile all around. At last we reached the top of a hill from where we could see with the naked eye the village and even the many bustling figures in it.

Upon our approach we greeted each other with the customary shot in the air and soon the entire population, under the command of the lesser chiefs, appeared before us while firing continuously in our honor. Dismounting, the chiefs approached us according to their rank and shook hands with us. This ceremony continued until we made friends with everyone and shook everyone's hand, during which time the chiefs stood next to us, like generals overseeing the movements of their troops.

Soon blankets, reeds, and pillows were brought, and in a matter of minutes tents were erected for our entire company and numerous blazing bonfires were crackling. They unsaddled our animals and took them to graze under the supervision of Indian shepherds. Our baggage was piled in a heap and was also guarded by an Indian.

Everything having been thus put in order, our entire company was led to the largest hut—the council house—in the village, where a feast was ready and waiting for us. All kinds of fish, cooked roots, shells, venison, mutton, and much more was dished out for us in large quantities. Needless to say we all did our best to do justice to this royal feast.

With the meal finished, the council session began. After smoking the peace pipe (the indispensable opening for every Indian council) the

chiefs as well as the entire tribe displayed particular curiosity about basic information concerning the United States, its people and government, of which they knew nothing, excepting the vague rumors received through their neighbors, the Tejon Indians. All their contacts and barter were only with Mexicans. I summoned all my eloquence to stress the virtues of the United States and particularly to make them understand the benefits of American friendship. My argument was elaborately supported by our friend the chief with the long name, and he has done everything to make his tribe understand the generosity of the people from the east, whose representatives and envoys their guests were. Both the chiefs and the people seemed to receive this intelligence with great joy and satisfaction and appeared eager to accept friendly relationship. I say "all the people" advisedly, for while only the chief warriors were present in the council house, the oratory was by no means restricted to this small group, for every sentence, point by point, was communicated loudly to the people gathered outside, by narrators standing at the doors. This custom of communicating with the people through narrators is not limited to the Mojave, but is found among many other Indian tribes. It must be admitted that it is an ingenious institution in places not yet ready for newspapers, and it is entirely just and fair to announce the results of the deliberations of the council, verbatim and on the spot, so that everyone may refute anything that is reported incorrectly. Unquestionably, this is right and is at least as accurate as the usual press communication.

These narrators are mostly older people who, because of their age, are no longer useful for anything else, and every village has these "walking newspapers"—as the white man calls them. They walk around and report the events of the day, town meetings, hunting parties, festivals, dances, and any other happening of public interest. In particular they announce anything lost or found by anyone. I lost my gloves while I was there, and before I had noticed it, they were taken to the chief and in no time a messenger appeared, carrying the gloves on a pole. He announced the found article and called for the owner to claim it.

How difficult it is to understand and study the true character of these savages! In his latest work Washington Irving states that the Mojave are inhospitable, selfish, and deceitful nomads and in general a despicable, thieving bunch.* Having been personally among them and

*Washington Irving, *Astoria*.

later having visited them several times from Tejon, I am convinced that they are friendly and hospitable people, honest to a fault, and unselfish in every respect, and going even further, I can state with assurance that although they are uneducated, heathen savages, one would have to go to the far corners of the earth to find a more open, honest, and unspoiled people.

Yesterday, the chief with the long name complained of a cough and a hoarse throat, so I gave him a stiff dose of powder and this morning another one, and by now he has completely recovered. This successful experiment made me so famous that they are certain they have the best doctor in the world and hordes of them crowd around me, asking for medicines. Greatly appreciating the confidence placed in me and weighing the possible profit to be derived from it, I tried, to the best of my ability, not only to maintain but to increase this inexpensively acquired confidence. Fortunately, I have reached the age when everyone is a doctor to some extent and was able to utilize the small healing tricks picked up during my travels and apply them successfully in a few simple cases. The only patient who ruined all my Aesculapian mixtures and discouraged any experimentation was a dried up, old crone with a terrible rasping cough. I could not help her at all, but tried to console her by promising to send her a good medicine from Tejon. The husband was so pleased with this assurance that he immediately offered a piglet for breakfast, which I accepted with thanks as an honorarium for my medical services.

July 17. Continuing our journey in the company of the chief with the long name, the time passed pleasantly, for our friend discoursed on every bush and spring *per longum et latum*, peppering his comments on nature with countless anecdotes. We were still traveling on the bank of the Mojave, and the ever-changing landscape was truly enjoyable. At times we advanced under steeply rising cliffs, then again we crossed meadows that seemed to be smiling at us; here and there we found ourselves in rolling valleys where our admiration was aroused by the beauty of the animal and plant life. In many places we met small bands of Mojave, and at such times we always stopped to shake hands. They were all curious to learn the purpose of our journey, and the chief with the long name was very helpful in satisfying this with his loquacious eloquence, explaining to everyone at length who and what we were.

Our chief's habit of accompanying his eternal chatter with constant puffs on his pipe has finally exhausted our tobacco supply, and thus it seemed that our friend Yumusruy-Ekahat-Hum was in danger of having to stop his prattle. But to our great amusement, we found we were mistaken, because without the slightest embarrassment and great ingenuity he chopped up half the reed stem of his pipe, stuffed his pipe with part of it and lit up again.

If we enjoyed the Mojave landscape, its branch called Nevajo (which we have just reached) filled us with genuine wonder. In places, frighteningly shaped, black rock columns of fabulous size incline over the river at great height like so many giant bastions and turrets. Here and there, gaping precipices and deep chasms yawn, which seem to tell of nature's upheaval in times past. In some places the river was quiet and smooth as a mirror; elsewhere it roared down over granite barriers with foaming, raging fury, rolling huge boulders along with a tremendous racket sounding like thousands of cannon shots.

In many places the boulders were strewn pell-mell, enough to stagger the imagination, while in other spots the narrow valleys strained under the burden of the lush vegetation. The grandeur of the region is such that it beggars the ability of the writer or the artist to describe or paint it. Nothing that we have seen on this trip is comparable to the Nevajo area. The traveler never ceases to wonder, for at every turn he is either terrified or filled with indescribable delight. I hardly believe that there is another river in North America whose surroundings are as unexpectedly rich and romantic as the Mojave and its tributaries. From its source in the Sierra Nevada to its junction with the great Colorado, the Mojave covers about 600 miles amidst areas of such fabulous variety that it defies the imagination. Its source is in the layers of debris of an extinct crater in a general area which has all the indications of the elements of primeval fires. As it leaves the Sierras, its course is over deserts of sand and lava; then it crosses many mountain chains, plunging down in awesome falls, while elsewhere its hardly noticeable flow snakes through smiling valleys and meadows.

Following the Nevajo, we had ascended to a considerable height when the chief stopped, dismounted, and asked us to take a break while he attended to some business with his nephew, who lived straight across the river in a cluster of huts. Hearing the old chief's yells, the nephew immediately jumped into a canoe and within a few minutes was amongst us. He was a handsome, strapping fellow, which his scanty clothing tended to emphasize. It consisted, according to Mojave custom, of a pair of short trunks made of rabbit skins. The chief with the long name introduced his nephew, who I regret to say had an equally long name—Hajse-i-Kaukau Miutiugetsh. Our new friend was particularly curious to find out who we were, where we came from, where were we going and for what purpose. All his questions were answered by his uncle with his usual verbose eloquence. By this time there was voluminous parleying going on between them and the Indians crowding on the opposite bank. Soon, many canoes were crossing over, filled with tobacco and a variety of foodstuffs for the journey which our new friend had also decided to join.

We spent the night in the most northeasterly Mojave village. We had a pleasant time in the midst of this kind and hospitable tribe. They offered to serve us in every way they could, and not only did they satisfy all our wishes but even tried to anticipate them.

The fame of my medical knowledge had reached here already. We had hardly arrived when the chief Opush Yje Cathum asked me to help his daughter, who had been sick for weeks and whom the Indian medicine men were unable to cure. I stepped into the hut and found the girl on a reed mat, suffering greatly from cramps. She seemed to be her father's particular favorite. He vowed eternal gratitude to the Americans should I cure the daughter. I would have done everything I could regardless of all this, for the girl's beauty and suffering aroused my sympathy. The only trouble was that I did not know what was wrong with her, and my medical knowledge was insufficient to determine the cause. After a good deal of pondering, as one always does when unsure of oneself, I had the girl placed in a steam bath (steam baths are very popular among California Indians for cleanliness) where she was kept sweltering to the point of prostration; then I administered a stiff dose of gunpowder dissolved in water, had her wrapped in a buffalo hide, and piled on a few hundredweights of buffalo and wolf skins, until she fell asleep.

Whether the reader believes it or not, the cure was a complete success, for by the morning the girl was well, past all danger, although still quite weak. Then I turned to homeopathy and ordered a solid week of fasting, save for a daily cup of venison broth.

The great chief was so overjoyed by his daughter's recovery that he forgot his dignity and turned handsprings and somersaults, and kept urging me to stay on as his guest, the longer the better. However, our mules were saddled, and were ready to push on. As my mule was brought forth, the chief exclaimed that it was undignified that an animal with such big ears should carry an important personage like myself and insisted quite forcefully in exchanging my mule for his best horse, remarking how happy he was seeing his friend on the back of this noble animal.

I want to observe that the above mentioned steam bath is very common among the Mojave Indians. They call them sweat huts and are small, tightly sealed shacks; the steam is produced by water dripping on glowing, redhot stones.

July 18. Leaving the land of Opus Yje Cathum, we entered the Tejon Indian territory, leaving behind the mountainous landscape. Our route was over gently rolling meadows so luxuriant, that one of our companions from Ohio claimed that he has never seen more fertile land. Toward noon we reached a tall forest. After crossing it, Lake Tulare loomed over the horizon, and by sunset we had arrived safely at our final destination, Fort Tejon.

Since we have praised the Mojave Indian so much, it is our regrettable duty to relate an incident which perhaps, even if temporarily, casts a cloud on their character. During our pleasant chat last night, one of my friends showed us a white rat from his collection, which the local hunters consider a valuable rarity. The Indians also were ogling it, examining it with amazement and claimed that the white rat's skin has unparalleled magic powers against any sickness when used as a head ornament. In the morning when we were about to start, the rat was missing. We searched everywhere but found no trace of it, so it was obvious that one of the Indians pilfered it. Both the village chief and the chief with the long name became very excited over this unpleasant incident and immediately called together the entire population to investigate it. Every single one of them, however, resentfully denied the charge, declaring that no one would dare to offend the generous Americans in this manner. The investigation was just about over when several Indians noticed the dog of the chief with the long name, who traveled everywhere with us, and emphatically asserted that the strange dog ate the precious white rat.

Everybody knows that when a dog is accused of a crime, it is usually immediately condemned and executed. This was now the case. The unfortunate dog was caught at once and its growl and snarl confirmed their suspicion, and so unanimously it was sentenced to death. In vain did my friend maintain that his dog never ate rats; in vain did I plead for mercy for the poor delinquent. The judges were relentless, for according to them the dog committed a double crime: stealing from friends, the "magnanimous" Americans, and beclouding Mojave honor and integrity. The poor animal was tied to a stake and shot full of arrows.

The sentence thus having been carried out, an autopsy was immediately performed to confirm the crime and remove any stain on the Mojave character. It goes without saying that everyone followed the procedure with much curiosity, but to our great dismay, there was no trace of the rat in the innards of the animal.

This unexpected result so infuriated the chief with the long name, that after some harsh words, bitter quarrels and threats, he started a general free-for-all. It took our armed intervention to calm down the brawling parties. After so doing, we enumerated the many natural causes which might account for the rat's disappearance, and we assured them that in no way did we suspect them. Although we had thus disposed of the matter, our friend with the long name was so disturbed over the affair that he changed his original plan to continue with us and, after an emotional farewell, went home.

Part II
Tejon and the Tejon Indians

The Indian affairs policy pursued for years by the United States was extended also to California. No sooner had a peace treaty been signed with Mexico than New Mexico, Arizona, and California became part of the Union. Agents were sent from Washington by the commissioner of Indian affairs with instructions to assemble all the Indians of the above territories, and persuade or if necessary (depending on the circumstances), force them to engage in agriculture. In general they were to be concentrated, tribe by tribe, in permanent settlements, thus opening up the huge territories over which until now, the Indians had been hunting and roaming. In general, safety of travel to these places was to be secured.

The agents were usually accompanied by soldiers who built one or more forts in the center of the tribal territories, partly to keep the Indians in check, should they resist the demands of the civilian authorities, and partly for the protection of travelers and settlers. If we set aside the fact that the building of each of these forts brought about the annihilation of some Indian tribes, then we must admit that these measures undoubtedly did much to promote the general welfare. Areas which hitherto the white man had not dared to penetrate and which therefore had been closed to civilization, were now occupied by large numbers of settlers as soon as the forts were built, and garrisoned. At first only the immediate vicinity of the forts was occupied; then people spread out further and further, until in a few years the forts were surrounded by flourishing settlements and townships.[3]

The settler enjoyed many advantages in these places. He could dispose of all his produce at very high prices to the garrison and the craftsmen serving it, for, in the beginning, there was no other means of obtaining food or any article of comfort, often for hundreds of miles. The European traveler is amazed, after crossing a thousand or more miles of desert where he has not seen a single white man, to stumble on a fort in the wilderness, surrounded by many flourishing settlements and towns, steam mills, furniture factories, smithies, newspresses, and so on, and he is able to secure not only the necessities, but also such articles and in abundance, as Havana cigars, French champagne, Panama hats, patent leather boots, fine porcelain and crystals. It is true that the prices of these articles are exorbitant, but no one is forced to buy them; if he does, let him think of the difficulties and hardships the merchant had to contend with, the breakage and spoilage in transporting these goods until they finally arrive here, in the wilderness.

It was in this fashion that Fort Tejon was established.* Near the fort a large valley (Canyon las Uvas or Grapevine Canyon) was chosen for an Indian settlement. Many of them did settle here, and at present they are diligently cultivating their fields, but the great majority would not hear of settling down and to this day are scattered all over, living an independent life of hunting, fishing, and so on. Here and there a few families jointly cultivate the land in the mountains.

The fort was established in 1854 in the so-called Canyon del Tejon mountain pass, in the most fertile, beautiful, and healthy part of the country. To the north of the mouth of the pass stretches Lake Tulare, on the shores of which grows exceptionally good grazing grass and there is also sufficient wood for building purposes.

Already three little towns have sprung up next to the lake in the immediate vicinity of the fort, and individual farmers in great numbers have settled for miles around. If the reader will recall our description of

*However plausible the term "fort" may be, the reader should not view it in the European sense. The American fort consists only of a few frame or brick buildings (often just tents), a few barracks, a few small buildings for the officers, a mill, a storehouse for food, arms, and clothing, and a hospital surrounded by gardens. There is no sign of fortification of any kind as there would be no need for it against spears and arrows. [This is Xántus's comment. Ed.]

the hardships of the journey (it is true that there are several easier routes than the one I chose, but they are all much longer and very few people use them), he will be astonished to learn that these newborn little townships already have coffeehouses complete with billiard tables, a few inns furnished in New York style, and stores where every imaginable article from Manchester cottonware to Brussels lace or Parisian carpets can be purchased. Not only are Strasbourg pâté and Genoa sardines available, but also ice cream of all kinds, although this latter at an exorbitant price. This is not surprising since ice has to be brought from a distance of 700 miles, and it is no wonder that it costs three dollars a pound.

To show that we are not behind the fashion, it is only necessary to mention one thing: the crinoline safely reached us last year, and right now there is not a single lady among us who is not cavorting in one. Last year there were much fewer grizzly bears and wolves than in previous years, and one lively wit firmly maintained that this was due to the crinoline, because bears and wolves were as scared of it as the Indians were of the camel. If this statement could be proved beyond a doubt, it would make the crinoline the most useful item in the world. Truly, last year, we could not walk a mile without being chased up a tree by a bear, regardless of whether or not we were accompanied by a lady, but now if we walked next to a crinoline we could not meet up with a bear even if we wanted to.

The Tejon Indians are a completely independent tribe. They occupy their mountainous territory, the extent of which is about 12,000 square miles, and if need be they can put 3,000* mounted warriors in the field.

The valleys in this mountainous country run in a south-north direction. There are deep gullies, steep crevices, and hazardous mountain passes in many places. These passes are the only routes on which one can travel in this land. The eastern side of the mountains is a comparatively gentle slope and it can be climbed with not too much difficulty. But the western and southern sides are very steep. In many places they are 5,000 and even 6,000 feet high. In general the tops of the mountains are flat plateaus or mesas. That is why, looking down from a mountain top, the entire area appears to consist of low hillocks. If, however, one looks toward the west, one sees steep, bastionlike

*Possible misprint.

mountain chains of sandstone formation, probably belonging to a more recent class of carboniferous sandstone. Ordinarily this stone is soft and crumbly, but occasionally one may find harder specimens suitable for building in this climate. Elsewhere, however, where the air is not so dry and the rate of evaporation is fast enough, they are unsuited for building purposes. There is also some limestone nearby, but due to its impurity, it is difficult to burn the lime out of it. It would have to be kept in kilns for ten to twenty-five days. Large quantities of debris and layers of excellent-quality mica can be seen everywhere. Here and there good quality coal and some pyrope also can be found.

There is evidence of gold everywhere, both in the water and on land, but the northern regions being so much richer in this precious metal, it is not profitable as yet to pan and mine it here, although in years to come mining may attain importance here, too.

At some places there are huge, 300- to 400-foot high mounds of lava visible. There is a curious lavalike flow in existence between the lower Tulare Lake and the Cajon Pass, which is about 200 yards wide and seventy miles long. The center of the volcano appears to have been on a peak named Mills, which is one of the tallest peaks in the area. It is visible from a distance of fifty miles and has two extinct craters. The aforementioned lava flow is undoubtedly of a more recent origin, for the waves, twists, and turns are still noticeable on the surface, although the Spanish exploratory expeditions that describe this area do not mention it, nor is there anything in the Indians' ancestral legacy that accounts for such an event.

On the northeastern border of the Tejon territory there are many signs indicating that not too long ago it was the scene of an enormous volcanic eruption. This was further corroborated by the diary of Hernandez on the exploration of southern California: "Continuing our route from the northwest corner of the Purple Sea toward the Pacific Ocean we soon reached a desert which was covered with hot ashes, so that it was impossible for us to continue, for the choice was either to drown in the Ocean or penetrate the ashes. The ground was vibrating and trembling like a huge drum and for this reason Father Anastasius was of the opinion that there were subterranean waters, perhaps a sea here; and in some places the ashes were flaming and smoking with a hellish roar." (*Exploration del California mas baxo*, by Enrico H. Hernandez, Madrid.)

The soil of the whole territory is mostly sandy, mixed in some places with gray clay, spongy and porous everywhere. Because of the lack of water it is not suitable for cultivation. After a rain, large areas are covered with soda crystals and agriculture is out of the question. The water is very hard and causes upset stomachs to those not yet accustomed to it. Upon my request, Dr. Bahr, a San Francisco chemist, analyzed the water at Fort Tejon, and found that it contained large quantities of limed carbonic acid, magnesium sulfide, sodium carbonate, and elements of potassium and sodium chlorides.

At the end of the winter, during the rainy season, the whole area is impassable, except on the well-trodden paths on the mountain ridges, on account of the sponginess of the soil. Almost everywhere, the mountains are covered with artemisia. No other plant, not even a blade of grass grows there, consequently the country resembles an unsightly desert. However, in the valleys where the creeks flow, the soil is fertile, with tropical fruits and vegetation.

For a long time this land was famous as an incomparable cattle-raising area. Gama grass, or sheep grass, which is eminently suitable for cattle grazing, grows on the mesas and foothills, and it is very nutritious, and just as green when cut and dried. All animals like it, especially horses. This gama grass does not, however, grow in such abundance in Tejon as outsiders may think, therefore, we may safely state, that the rumors about the economic capacity of the land are much exaggerated, and we are convinced that if the present stock would double in number, many would starve to death. For example, the annual supply of hay required for the horses (fifty-four) of a company of dragoons at Fort Tejon, is the crop of an area of fifty square miles, and ordinarily even that is not sufficient. The government pays eighty-five dollars for a ton of hay of such inferior quality that no one in the western states would accept it even for free. Therefore, the fame of the Tejon territory as a cattle-raising country is a myth, originated perhaps by transients, hastily passing through, or by haphazard Mexican hearsay, for exactly the opposite is the fact.

Pines, dwarf oaks, cacti of great variety (sixty-five) and palms make up the flora of the valleys. Here and there cedars can be seen on the mountain slopes, where the artemisia is not native. Exceptionally tall and slender pines may be found in the deep mountain passes and poplars at the edge of swamps. Around the Kern River I saw a few acacias which were burdened with very beautiful carmine red flowers, but acacias are actually rare.

Gooseberry, plum, raspberry, grape, and especially hops grow in immense quantities on the creek banks, also a certain species of dwarf willow (*Salix cascarilla Xantus - Botanical Memoir of Southern California* [Philadelphia, 1858]), the hair of which the Indians use instead of tobacco—which is not only an excellent substitute for tobacco, but has such agreeable scent and taste, that it would be good enough for the shah of Persia.

The winter is normally short and if it were not for the rainy season, it would not even be noticeable, for the temperature is often as high as 95° in December and January. It is shirt-sleeve weather throughout the winter. During the rains, the ground becomes a veritable quagmire, which quivers like jelly when one treads on it. This, however, does not last long, for soon everything becomes parched again with the onset of the dry season. In the spring the wind blows continuously from the south and southwest, and the air is laden with so much dust that it is unpleasant to travel. The winter and spring rains also come from the south and southwest.

In the summer the heat is not unbearable, unless one is exposed to the vertical rays of the sun. The nights, without exception, are cool and pleasant and a blanket or cover is always needed. The greatest rainfall is in February. It starts raining in January and ends in the middle of March. In June all vegetation becomes parched wherever there is no water, partly because the porous soil absorbs all moisture, and partly due to the high altitude; the rate of evaporation is very fast and so all vegetation suffers from the lack of moisture.

The meteorological table below best illustrates the climate of Tejon and Southern California. I have prepared this table by governmental order for the Patent Office and it can be considered official in every respect. For those unacquainted with the technique of meteorological observations, the table clearly shows that statistics were taken three times daily of temperature, wind direction, and weather, and daily and monthly medians were arrived at by appropriate calculations.

To measure the rainfall, we had a brass funnel made, which was placed on a pyramid-shaped stand far removed from any object which could obstruct the free fall of the rain. After each rain, the accumulated water was measured with an imbibometer (rain gauge) which was calibrated from ten inches to 1/100 of an inch, thus we were able to measure the rainfall over an area of fifteen-and-one-half square miles by a funnel with a diameter of ten-and-one-half inches.

The area suitable for cultivation in the Tejon district is very

Table A Transcript of the minutes of the meteorological station established at Canyon de la Uvas, between June 1857 and June 1858 (1 year).

Year and Month	Fahrenheit				Wind								Weather		Rain Fall
	7:00 AM	2:00 PM	9:00 PM	Median	North	North East	East	South East	South	South West	West	North West	Clear	Cloudy	Inches and 1/100's inches
													Day		
1857															
June	71	85	77	77	4	12	14	16	25	6	9	4	29	1	
July	72	89	78	79	5	5	11	22	10	3	26	11	31	0	
August	75	85	76	75	6	14	6	19	8	18	12	10	28	3	
Sept.	64	79	73	72	13	6	0	8	10	31	18	4	29	1	
Oct.	59	76	64	66	5	6	8	6	11	21	19	17	30	1	
Nov.	53	69	60	60	2	0	0	7	9	19	34	19	27½	2½	0.15
Dec.	49	59	54	54	10	16	1	0	0	18	32	16	25⅓	5⅔	0.45
1858															
Jan.	45	54	50	49	0	0	0	0	0	46	43	4	15	16	2.85
Feb.	46	52	49	49	2	0	3	12	0	30	25	12	3	25	9.73
March	54	69	63	62	10	0	0	0	50	22	10	1	24	7	5.43
April	59	70	64	64	2	0	0	0	22	31	16	19	26	4	0.34
May	65	78	74	71	12	0	0	0	30	31	19	1	29	2	
Total					71	59	43	90	175	276	263	118	297⅓	68⅓	18.95

limited if the size of the territory is taken into consideration and I doubt very much that—with the exception of southern California—one can find a territory in North America of comparable size, with such a low percentage of arable land.

In view of the fact that there is no rainfall for nine months of the year, that there is seldom water in the rivers, and that the entire region is 7,000 feet above sea level, where the rate of evaporation is exceptionally fast, it is obvious that agriculture is possible only on a very limited scale. Occasionally the Indians grow a very small crop without irrigation by planting the seeds ten to twelve inches deep, which they can easily do in the friable soil, without shutting off air from the seeds. The only crops they plant are maize, wheat, squash, and different kinds of beans. Sometimes wheat is planted in rows, ten to fifteen grains in a hole, much like the way maize is planted in Hungary.

Although in many places in the valleys—as for example in Fort Tejon—olives, figs, oranges, and pineapple, as well as various plantains and melons grow fairly well, still, taking the entire area as a whole, no other fruit grows but peaches which, however, thrive in amazing quantity and quality, and many Indians subsist on them from June to October.

Nothing can be found out from these Indians about their origin. In response to my questioning, some of them stated with perfect seriousness, that they grew out of the soil like mushrooms or squash, while others assured me that they knew nothing of their origin and I did not doubt that they were right. One intelligent and credible Tejon chief told me, however, that his tribe is by no means pure blooded, but is to a great extent mixed with Utah, Arapahoe, Mojave, and Hopi Indians, so that it would be a difficult task to find a pure-blooded Tejon. Nor would it be easy to give a physiological description that would be applicable to the entire population. All the same, a pure-blooded Tejon Indian would have the following characteristics: tall (about six feet) with a well-proportioned body; prominent cheekbones, long and straight nose, high but receding forehead, hair and eyes, black; beautiful white teeth; thick lips and disproportionately large ears. The external appearance of the Tejon Indian would indicate that although from the standpoint of spiritual development he is inferior to the Caucasian race in many respects, he stands in first place among American aborigines.

Concerning their form of government, it has so little resemblance to any organized form that anarchy best describes it. They have neither hereditary nor elected chiefs, and the one who presently fills this office acquired it without popular choice. The emblems of the office are a silver breastplate and a long staff with a silver knob.

The authority of the chief thus installed in the office is naturally merely nominal, and should he act against the wishes of the majority, his power would be quickly broken. Almost everyone who owns a few horses, mules, or sheep considers himself important enough to demand a voice in the discussions of the council. But even those who by virtue of their wealth or bravery achieve popularity and respect proceed with caution in the council, lest they be held responsible for a decision or ruling which perhaps may not be to the liking of the majority of the tribe.

The junta, or governing council, is constituted therefore of the wealthiest, and every member is a self-appointed representative of the entire nation. The natural consequence of this arrangement is that the decision of the junta is never considered valid unless it is in accord with the wishes of the majority of the people, and because of this, very few decisions are made or implemented. The absence of a popularly chosen chief with unlimited authority to rule is unquestionably to the disadvantage of this tribe, and makes its control and governance very difficult. It would take no little tact to suggest this, for it would meet with much uproar and antagonism, as they are thoroughly convinced that they are the most powerful nation on earth. This unfortunate belief may have originated from the fact that for many years they were the object of dread and terror of the northern Mexican states, due to their successful invasions and plunder. The wealthiest are now beginning to believe that the U.S. dragoons are far from being terrified by the mere mention of their name, but this belief is not yet widespread among the poorer class, which is the majority, and does not own horses, mules, or sheep. For this reason, they often attack travelers even today, and more than once drive off the herds of white settlers. The chief is so powerless to prevent these aggressive acts and to capture and punish the perpetrators, that many times he would rather compensate for the damages and destruction out of his own fortune than try to recover the stolen property.

In short, the Tejon governmental system cannot be considered a proper government at all, as everyone does what he pleases, due to the chief's lack of authority. If it were not for the fear of the dragoons, complete anarchy would prevail.

Around Fort Tejon and in the valley of de las Uvas (grape vine valley), there are many nice houses in good condition owned by those who have settled here and now live under the supervision of the commissioner. Taken as a whole however, one must state that their dwellings consist of temporary tents only, of the most primitive construction. They are of sugarcone shape, built of twigs and poles, covered with leaves or weeds, and in most of them a man of medium height cannot stand erect. A hole on the side, covered with sheep or deerskin and sometimes with blankets, serves as a door. A shack like this is unquestionably warm enough during the winter rains, but all in all it is very uncomfortable because it completely shuts out fresh air.

On the eastern slopes of the Sierra Nevada many of the Tejons live in caves among the rocks, and possibly this is what the scientist, Dr. Wagner, meant when he stated in his work that the Tejon Indians live in "beautiful stone houses." *"Sie lebe in wahrhaft schonen und geschmackvollen steinernen Hausern uberall"* (*Reise im Westlichen Amerika*).[3] They do not build anything that could be called houses, for all of them live in the above described shacks and they do not come within a shadow of that high degree of civilization with which many travelers credit them when they claim that "they stand in first place among American Indians as to the standard of dwelling places," because we can unhesitatingly state that they are far behind the Indians of the northwest.

One of the oddest customs of the Tejon Indians is that when someone dies, the rest of the family immediately abandons the shack and under no circumstances can they or anyone else be persuaded to occupy it again.

Steam baths are also commonly used by these Indians. A four-foot-high hut is constructed for this purpose, the frame fitted with a quantity of sheepskin. The user enters the hut, stuffs the hole—alias door—with a sheepskin, and drops cold water on preheated stones placed in the hut ahead of time. In a few minutes he perspires so profusely that water drips from his entire body.

The Indians' clothing is varied. Many wear short, brown, deerskin drawers resembling swimming trunks, while others wear woolen pants trimmed with red or dark red galloons. Sometimes these uncomfortable clothes are supplemented with some gaudy feathers, or long, colored blades of grass suspended from a string tied around the waist. Their footwear consists of deerskin moccasins, as with all other

73

11. *Tejon Indian Women Grinding Maize*, original drawing by John Xántus, 1858; print by Haske & Co., Pest, 1859

American Indians. During cold or rainy weather they wear a blanket with a hole cut in the center through which they stick their head. The blanket thus serves as a cape and it is not only a useful but also a decorative and tasteful piece of garment. The Tejon Indians call it *baize.*

Necklaces and bracelets are very fashionable, and from them one can normally judge the wearer's economic status. The wealthy wear Mexican and Peruvian doubloons, eagles and half eagles strung on a cord; not long ago we saw a necklace constructed of doubloons and double eagles weighing six-and-one-quarter pounds and worth $875. The middle class is contented with silver coins and the poorest with goat, lynx, and badger teeth.

These are the only articles of clothing worn by these Indians; during the summer whole bands, both men and women, can often be seen without any clothing but moccasins and bracelets. Last winter I met up with a hunting party whose total and only clothes consisted of their moccasins, even though the thermometer stood at 36° (Fahrenheit). This footwear is of fine quality, made of cured, dark brown deerskin, except for the soles, for which ox, pig, or horsehide is used. The leg reaches six inches above the ankle and is identical for both sexes.

The female apparel consists, aside from the above described moccasin, of colorful feathers or tall grasses of many hues hanging from a string around the waist; following a more recent fashion, however, they also use gaudy colored blankets which are sewn in the form of a skirt reaching only to the knee or even shorter, à la Lola Montez. Now it is appropriate to mention that the women ride exactly as the men, with or without saddle.

No kind of headgear or headress is known among these Indians. In the coldest of winters or the hottest of summers, rain or shine, both men and women go barehead. Both sexes grow their hair long which hangs down their back and is often four, even four and one-half feet long. It is an amusing sight to see it swinging back and forth like the tail of a cat, especially when they are on horseback. The writer of these lines being of the present generation has naturally no memory of the times of Marie Theresa and the Emperor Joseph, and it was therefore a rare experience to witness a sight among these Indians reminiscent of the appearance of Hungarian patriots and warriors in those wondrous days.

But, to return to our topic, we must mention that the Tejon Indians in general suffer from acute rheumatism, which often deteriorates into a chronic condition, when of course it becomes quite serious. Gonorrhea and syphilis are also not uncommon. They try to cure every sickness with steam baths and assorted herbs, and if these are unavailing, as a last resort they turn to dancing, chanting and sorcery. Women in labor stand upright holding on to a rope or staff hung above their heads, sometimes they also kneel, but the torso always stays in upright position. This method results in quick and painless births, although in exceptional cases the opposite is true, when, to achieve a successful outcome, they resort to chanting, dancing, smoking, and earsplitting drumming.

The dominant item in their diet is maize, which they mix with pumpkinseed before it ripens, crush, place into pumpkin hair and bake in hot ashes. Most of the maize, however, is left on the stalk until it is completely ripe, then the kernels are carefully removed and stored in underground pits for the winter. Before using, they mill it and make flour out of it. This is time-consuming and hard work, for first the maize is put into a stone-lined trough, and then ground with huge, square grindstones. This is strictly a feminine chore. If one realizes that one woman can produce no more than five pounds of flour, from morning till night, the conclusion is inevitable that these poor women spend half their lives grinding maize, and that is actually the fact.

It would be difficult to describe what the Tejons eat beside the aforementioned bread, for they eat anything and everything they can get their hands on. Hamsters, owls, crows, buzzards, dogs, horses, cats, weasels, and so on, are part of their everyday diet. They also eat all kinds of fruit, berries (including acorns), and I even saw them feast on rotting carrion, the sight of which was enough to turn our stomachs. A rattlesnake is a particularly choice morsel for them. They cut the head off, skin it, and bake it on glowing embers, just like an eel.

The main occupation of the entire nation is sheep and horse raising. The number of sheep is estimated between 10,000 to 400,000. In my opinion it is around 250,000.* The wool of the Tejon sheep is coarse, similar to that of the Hungarian sheep from Baranya, and they are never sheared. One of their peculiarities is that in every herd there are many four- and even six-horned specimens. The rams are with the

*An unrealistic estimate.

ewes throughout the year, so the ewes yean all the time, with the result that during the rainy season many lambs perish. This is the reason why the herds do not multiply as much as people think if they are not familiar with the conditions of the land. Goats are also numerous, grazing together with the sheep.

Spinning and weaving are done by the women, exclusively by hand, and for this reason the thread is usually coarse and of uneven thickness. Blanket weaving is a long and arduous task, as it is for the San Fernando Indians. Blankets woven in this manner are coarse, thick, and heavy, without a nap and are inferior to the ordinary American or English blankets. Nevertheless, some Tejon blankets are so tightly woven that water cannot penetrate them. At first I would not believe this, but after an experiment I was convinced that many gallons of water can be carried on horseback to a distance of forty or fifty miles without losing a drop, if it is properly tied up. But this unusual quality is of little advantage in daily usage, for during the rains the blankets absorb so much water that their great weight is a heavy load on the poor traveler. The Tejons' favorite colors are red, blue, black, and yellow; black and red braids are the most common. Red dye is made from the hair of Mazquanita (*Yucca acutifolia* Torrey), black from the wool of black sheep, blue from indigo sap, yellow from the flowers of the tulip tree (*Lyriodendron tulipifera* Linn.) The colors are usually woven in stripes, braids, and squares, but I never saw complicated or intricate patterns.

Very rarely, however, one does find some quite showy blankets of very fine weave which fetch fabulous prices, often as much as $100 and even $125. These are seldom made, or only for a very specific purpose, or else when commissioned to fill an individual order. Two to three women work six and many times eight whole months to produce such a blanket. Even so, the Tejons themselves prefer to wear American-made blankets because they are cheap and light, and even more so because the Americans cater to their customers' taste, and weave and dye the blankets to conform to Tejon fashion.

Still, there is one advantage to the Tejon blanket which should not go unmentioned: under open skies, in a bivouac, it can serve as a bed. Because of its tight weave, moisture or fog does not penetrate it and it stays perfectly dry. No other blanket can boast of this feature, and I believe it is due to the peculiarity of the weave which is entirely original and known only to these Indians. This specialty, connected with their magnificent ruins and architectural remains, indicating a high degree of civilization, gave rise to the opinion that the Tejons are probably the remnants of ancestral Mexican Indians, the Aztecs and the Tuscaloosa.

Their horses number about 80,000. Undoubtedly, they are descendants of the horses the Spaniards brought and interbred with local strays. The Spanish bloodline is recognizable even today. In breeding, the mares are completely ignored and neglected, only the stallions are cared for, as they believe that the quality of the offspring depends on the quality of the stallion. The horses in general are of short stature, although handsome and good runners. There are Tejon horses on which one can gallop 100 miles without a lengthy rest stop, and they will not falter. But after such an exertion the horse must be put to pasture at once and cannot be used for months.

The Tejon saddle is very similar to the Mexican and Central American saddle and it may be safely concluded that it is also of Spanish origin, except that the Tejon uses a longer stirrup strap and a much shorter stirrup than the Mexican. The bridle has a steel ring bit which encloses part of the horse's jaw and which exerts tremendous pressure, so that even the balkiest horse can be checked when the reins are pulled. Small steel slices, silver coins, and metal shives dangle from both sides of the bridle, which produce a tinkling sound so that one can hear a Tejon approaching one-half mile away. The check-rein and saddle are decorated with deerskin fringes which almost sweep the ground. They are also ornamented with porcupine quills and parrot feathers and sometimes with large disks and spheres of pure silver. (It is noteworthy that the Tejons are experts in judging the purity of silver. Even at a superficial glance, they can tell whether the metal is pure or alloyed with copper or other base metals.)

The greatest merit of their horses is unquestionably their surefootedness. Often they climb steep mountains with their masters on their back and gallop on such narrow paths that the onlooker's hair stands on end, but a mishap is unheard of, or at any rate a very unusual occurrence. I rode more than once on these animals on mountains with a grade of 60° or even steeper without any trouble.

However, in general, I think that those who contend that these horses surpass the eastern ones from the standpoint of beauty and utility are wrong. Rather, the very opposite is true. Their stature, endurance, and usefulness are definitely inferior to the horses of eastern America. A stout and beautiful horse is very exceptional and if in a stud of hundreds of horses one finds two or three good ones, this only proves how mistaken and ridiculous this contention is.

To be truthful, I cannot say that the Tejons are a diligent lot. While they grow some garden vegetables and cereals and raise horses and sheep, they are far from industrious. Like all other Indians, they do not work more than it is absolutely necessary to maintain themselves. I hold that if laziness or idleness is substituted for the meaning of the word industry, it would be more appropriate describing their character.

It is also untrue that they make butter and cheese. These two articles are extremely rare in a Mexican household. Knowing that Tejon ideas of civilized life are derived from their contact with Mexicans and the fact that they do not have cows, it stands to reason that they make neither butter nor cheese. Very rarely one sees cattle and therefore cows, and in such cases the Indians make an awful tasting and dreadful smelling round shaped something that resembles the national cheese of Germany (limburger). I do not believe that any part of the civilized world would call this horrid concoction cheese, although it is possible that our friend Mr. Wagner, the scientist, is of a contrary view, carried away by his national fervor.

As we have mentioned before, the Tejons were the objects of fear and terror in Mexico and New Mexico for almost a century-and-a-half, and every time they showed themselves in these lands, the population would flee for their lives, leaving all their earthly possessions behind. The mere rumor of their approach was sufficient for the people to sound the tocsin, fall on their knees, praying to their patron saints; they would sprinkle holy water on the fire, walk barefoot in processions, fast, and so on. In fact, even their litany was changed to include supplication against the Tejon incursions. Not long ago I saw a prayer book printed in La Paz in 1802. Every paragraph of the litany ended with "Save us oh Lord from the Tejon" and "Thwart the Tejon attack, oh Lord." Shepherds deserted their herds on their approach and naughty children were frightened by the mention of Tejon. But ever since the North American Union occupied the land, the fear of the Tejon ceased, even among the Mexicans. Undoubtedly, the fame of the Tejons' exceptional bravery was not due so much to their courage, but to the unheard-of cowardice of the Mexicans. While Mexico was a Spanish colony, the Tejons were not only kept in check, but often Spanish

79

armies invaded their heartland under the leadership of Jesuits and committed monstrous cruelties. It is no wonder that the Tejons took advantage of the troubled times between the end of the Spanish rule and the beginning of the American occupation and, observing that the populace was too cowardly to resist their raids, carried out the pillage and destruction of Mexico with increasing fury and savagery. They have not only kidnapped women and children, but once occupied even the capital city of New Mexico, Santa Fe, captured and tied up the governor of the province and took him with them as a prisoner. How matters have changed since the American occupation is best illustrated by the fact that the present garrison of Fort Tejon, a squadron of dragoons, is capable of maintaining order and keeping in check the entire nation of 300 mounted warriors.

The commonly used weapons of the Tejons are the bow and arrow and the spear with a long haft, and they are experts in their use. The bow is approximately four feet long and is made of a wood not found in Tejon territory but must be acquired through barter from the Apache Indians. The entire bow is covered with deerskin, partly to make it more flexible and partly to prevent cracks and breakage. The arrow is a yucca switch two feet long, with points of sharp chiseled steel or porcupine quill, although sometimes fish bone is also used for this purpose, with the most dangerous effect. The spear is ten feet long including the tip, which is eighteen inches long, and with a piece of steel honed to three edges and a sharp point tied to the haft with deerskin.

Should war break out it would be very difficult to defeat these Indians, not because of their valiant fighting, but because of their thorough knowledge of the countless number of caves and impenetrable mountain passes, which they could use to their advantage. However, although their cowardice is proverbial by now, it is by no means certain that they would not stand up and fight their enemies if they had to or if it became inevitable for their defense; and since they are convinced of being the mightiest nation on earth, it must be assumed that they would fight at least until the opposite is proven. Many of them possess firearms which they have acquired from fur traders before the American occupation, but they have not quite mastered their use as yet, and carry them more for ornament than utility.

There is very little known of their religion and the responses to my repeated inquiries seem to indicate that they have no conception of religion. Furthermore, there is no word in the Tejon language for

"Creator" or "Supreme Being." In the distant past the Jesuits carried on their missionary work here too, indicated by the wooden crosses, saints, readers, and pictures left behind. After their departure all traces of their activities vanished, and the pictures and figures of saints are valued by the Indians only as ornaments. I saw not long ago, in the home of a chief, an *Agnus Dei*, carved of wood, with the customary flag in the background, and asked him if he knew the meaning of the carving. He then related at length that the "sheep" lived at one time in the far south and a famous Tejon warrior brought it here from his distant campaign, and all Tejon sheep and goats are the descendants of the sheep and that is why the entire nation holds the "carved sheep" in great esteem. I was never able to find any ceremony resembling a divine service, and everyone who knows them well assured me that in this respect they are inferior to all other American Indians, and accordingly their ethical sense is limited. One can never count on the veracity of their statements. They are capable of the most outrageous lies if they think they could profit by it.

Lying therefore is a very common vice among the Tejon and thievery is not rare either. This latter vice has become so widespread that they often steal just for the sake of stealing. They would appropriate anything they can lay their hands on, whether they can use it or not. This I can state after many personal experiences. Not believing it at first, I have put them to the test. I left several of them alone in my room, and one of them stole my suspenders, another my doorknob, a third the key to my watch, another the frame of my mosquito netting, and still another stole a few strands of Spanish wax. The habit of stealing is so prevalent among them that the wife steals from her own husband and the husband from the wife. Not long ago, a chief asked the commander of Fort Tejon for permission to keep his horses under guard at the military stable, as rustling had become so prevalent that he would soon lose them all, while another prominent Indian asked the captain of the dragoons to punish one of his shepherds who was selling his horses and whom he was reluctant to punish because of his popularity in the tribe.

From all this it becomes evident how slanted is the claim—by that often mentioned author—that complete honesty prevails among the Tejons, due to the deterring effect of very strict laws. If such laws do actually exist, which we have grounds to doubt, they exist only on paper, for their practical effects are nowhere visible.

As I mentioned before, morality is also a very rare commodity among the Tejons. Husbands must ceaselessly guard their wife or wives, lest they stray from the straight and narrow path, and in spite of this, they often do. Women have great influence, far greater than in any other Indian nation in North America. The rearing of children is entirely their domain and they would never tolerate the father punishing the child. As a matter of fact, when I questioned a Tejon about this, he replied that he is afraid even to admonish his son, lest at a later occasion, the son might take his revenge and, upon the urging of his mother, shoot him full of arrows. Furthermore, the husband has no right at all to the property of his wife; their herds are kept and guarded separately, and this is probably at the origin of their influence, which extends not only to the home but to public affairs and is often exercised.

Women are bought from the father and always paid for by horses. There is no ceremony and if, after a two-week trial period, she is not satisfied with her husband she returns to her father, and that is the end of the affair. Polygamy is universal. Everyone can keep as many wives as he can pay for, but the wives do not necessarily live in the same hut, often not even in the same vicinity.

Inheritance is never from father to son, but to a younger brother, and in the absence of one, to his sister, and so it can happen that upon the death of a very rich father the sons could become beggars. If, however, the father distributes his wealth among his children during his lifetime, regardless of whether it was acquired or inherited, it is considered valid and accepted by all.

Prisoners taken in battle are usually treated with consideration and kindness, so much so, that those kept for a few years prefer to stay with them, even if the opportunity arises to go free and return to their home. Here and there one might escape or leave when given his freedom, but he is the exception, for usually the prisoners are worthless vagabonds and a burden on all.

The Tejons are very hospitable; they never ask their guests who they are or where they come from but provide them with all the comforts. To be truthful, one cannot say that they are cruel. It is possible or even probable that they do not consider killing a man soul-shaking, if the deed serves a purpose or they profit by it, but I do not believe them to be capable of killing a man for the enjoyment or sport of it, as so many other Indians do.

They passionately love dancing and often get together for that purpose. They also enjoy a variety of sports, horseracing and the game of dice. This latter is so widespread among them that many would risk their life's earnings on the throw of dice.

Their language, I think, is the most difficult among all Indian tongues and in my opinion the reason is not the complicated structure, but that the Tejons swallow or bite off the last syllable of their words, which makes it very hard to decipher the complete word and its origin. For months I took great pains to research the character of the Tejon language and had achieved considerable progress. I found that the Hungarian letters are perfectly adequate to clearly reproduce every Tejon word or sound. There are no genders in the language.

The numbers are as follow:

1 Nast		13 Mahtoti nah		
2 Nish		20 Neso		
3 Nah		21 Neso nast		
4 Nev		30 Navo		
5 Nohu		40 Nevo		
6 Nasoto		50 Nono		
7 Nesoto		60 Nasoto no		
8 Nanoto		70 Nesoto no		
9 Soto		80 Nanoto no		
10 Mahtoti		90 Soto no		
11 Mahtoti nast		100 Mahtoto no		
12 Mahtoti nish		101 Mahtoto no nast		

Thousands are expressed as ten times so many hundreds, for example ten, twenty, thirty times one hundred for 1,000, 2,000, or 3,000 (*Mahtoti mahtotono–Neso mahtotono–Navo mahtotono*).

Gradation of adjectives is expressed by using a diminutive or an expanding word qualifier before them, but the adjectives themselves are unchanged. Verbs are used in all tenses, but in one person only.

To acquaint the reader with the sound of the Tejon language, I list the following most common words:

Shell	minne	Shield	hiah
Clay	slick	Dance	matoto uteh
Canoe	rinmone	Drum	onne arom
Axe	kekoi anano	Singing	manis tutch
Flour	pini hakon	Frog	aunhi
Fish	hei iuk	Quiver	istis
Spit	ho mohu	Tree	aust

English		English	
Grass	most	Butterfly	avu chim
Bush	heki aust	Insect	ami kome
Foot race	ono schi	Spider	vinohe
Fire	oist	Tallow	irchki
Firewood	moist	Mirror	amvuam tutu
Pearl	oni avo kist	Orange	mu utavi
Sword	hunath	Thorn	is ku
Comb	tehine	Rattlesnake	shishi nuhu
Owl	nistah	Rope	shub hau
Bullet	vilmah	Cactus	matehetz
Iron	makeit	Pineapple	leip
Skin	wutan	Fig	etuk
Egg	wu wut	Peach	memi milk
Red	wiu mitoru	Lizard	hau tevich
Stone	aus chim	Gopher	isti hemeik
Duck	siski sum	Fan palm	huinus tik
Ashes	pahi	Sunflower	hei nuhuk
Coal	huhus	Otter	metchkuu
Blood	mihi	Grindstone	moi suka
Dew	ishi im mu	Steel	hu pasi
Leaf	wi putz pu	Cough	mai mitz
Root	otu muhiu	Rifle	mitunu
Whiskey	Wiok magpi	Heart	hivith
Turtle	meinek	Bone	oku nutz
Soldier	notak	Fear	tutatu ist
Chief	vihu	Club	omi
Goose	ennhi	Drinking cup	mahen
Justice	nitor	Hair	mik
Salt	wu pumah	Hill	pui ius
Marrow	alm	Mountain	omei mi
Mouse	oki	Marriage	ovistavan
Knife	mutaki	Intestine	wi eu nist
Road	mio	Watersnake	nihi chikis
Footpath	heki mio	Fly	meuchkis
Blanket	horn	Bee	henome
Hamster	mini vakeli	Centipede	mi chim mi
Deer	mah ha eh	Plum	miu nimim
Porcupine	makku	Gooseberry	sesu nitem
Bear	nakku	Melon	kuku natsi
Antelope	wukke	Maize	vuke namik
Hen	kuku iakine	Arrow	manuki
Grasshopper	hakote	Bow	otuvachi

Verbs:

English		English	
Shoot	otei hoi ist	Ride	poni voni
Cover	nino vist	Hide	im humi

84

Bake	en mututz	Hunt	ishi humuk
Cook	ishi vut	Lie down	raytu muik
Wrap	ippu ust	Sleep	sheku muik
Break	eyi utz		

In trying to paint an authentic picture of the Tejon, I must often disagree with some writers about the customs and life style of these people. Recently they have been presented in a manner that would do credit to any civilized nation from the standpoint of industry, moral character, and intelligence (*Transactions of the American Ethnological Society*, vol. II [Buffalo, N.Y., 1852–1853]). However none of these claims would stand up, for while it may be possible to find a few individuals among them who are trustworthy and intelligent (considering always that they are Indians), I would not advise anyone to depend unconditionally upon the integrity and benevolence of the Tejon.

The total lack of traditions is truly astonishing. They have no knowledge whatever about their origin or national history. If they are in fact the remnants of a great nation, which at one time in Mexico had a high degree of civilization (we mean the Aztecs), then they have sunk to such a low level that they are unrecognizable. Although enough conjectures and theory are surfacing today, the entire subject is still shrouded in mystery. Similarities were supposedly found in places where there were no indications of the slightest clue. Ancient ruins—presumably of Spanish origin—were explored to verify the story. Fragments of pottery were examined minutely under microscope and sketched, and then presented as memorabilia of Aztec culture of the past, although such specimens can be acquired by any scientist, in any quantity, by stepping into the first Tejon hut and buying a pitcher or pot for a half-real and smashing it to pieces. For all these reasons, I believe that the enthusiasm over the history and culture of the Aztec people and especially the resting places during their wanderings, has taken a turn of which one must disapprove, because a comparative study of the living Tejon language with the Aztec of antiquity is the only correct method to substantiate the claims, if that is at all possible, and which I have fundamental reasons to doubt.

There is nothing to be learned on this subject from the Tejons, for, as mentioned previously, they have no traditions. It is true that thick volumes could be written about anecdotes related by interpreters, but such a collection would be useless in probing the history of the nation due to their inconsistencies. If it is true that at one time they produced vessels of exquisite beauty and splendor, they certainly do not possess the secret of this art at present, for their output cannot stand the most lenient criticism. Since they do not grow wool, they do not make woolen fabric and they have never even heard of the enchanting featherstitch weave. Having lived among these people for close to a year, I had ample opportunity to get to know them and I have never seen among their artifacts (which, by the way, are quite limited in number) any that would even remotely resemble those produced by the ancient Aztecs, which are quite well-known. It can be stated with certainty that whatever insignificant handicrafts they do create were learned from the Spaniards.

Scientists eager to find the origin or remains of the great Aztec people rushed through the Tejon territory, and in their imagination peopled the scattered ruins found there with these people of antiquity, and in general attributed the common origin of different Indians to facts and customs which could be equally applied to the entire human race.

As I stated before, my opinion is that the kinship of peoples, if it does exist in fact, can only be ascertained by the study of their language. Customs, life style, the quality of artifacts, or the questioning of the Indians will not get one very far, in fact one cannot completely succeed at all. It takes no little effort and patience to persuade a Tejon to admit—against his will—that he is convinced that Montezuma will soon be among them, and that in certain caves they maintain an eternal flame in his honor. The Tejons in general do not trust the white man and one must be cautious in questioning them if one expects to get satisfactory answers, otherwise the Tejon will see through one in a minute and know what kind of answer is expected of him and respond accordingly.

If it is really true that they maintain and guard eternal flames in their caves—which, incidentally, I do not believe—then this custom, to which such great importance is attributed, by the same token could just as rightfully be compared with that of the Persians or Romans. As everyone who is familiar with world history knows, in different lands and at different times there were countless nations that maintained sacred fires. One cannot construct a theory on this custom alone.

In many places throughout the Tejon territory many hieroglyphics are to be found carved on the walls of caves and on slabs of rock in the mountain passes. These are also used to prove that the Tejon are descendants of the Aztec nation. I have carefully copied one such

12. *Indian Hieroglyphics in Cajon Pass, California,* unsigned

hieroglyphic in the Cajon Pass; the dimensions of the original slab are twenty-nine feet in length by thirteen-and-one-half feet in height.

It is my opinion that these hieroglyphics also are not too reliable. The execution of most carvings is quite crude, and most probably was done for pastime and amusement. To claim that these hieroglyphics may relate to the secrets of the past, present, or future history is in my view utterly ridiculous.

Newly discovered land and newly discovered people fire up the imagination of some who see them for the first time. This is the case also in the present situation. Not too long ago Tejon and its population were *terra incognita* and when civilization stumbled upon them, many pointed to them saying, "Lo, here are the descendants of the Aztec, and their resting place, after their wandering." No wonder, since the history of the Aztec and Toltec nations is still covered with the mist of time, the historian in his frantic eagerness will grasp every opportunity to build a forest out of a blade of grass and an ocean out of a few drops of water, for the instruction of the gullible masses.

Part III

The California Peninsula

In February 1858, half-way through his stay at Fort Tejon, Xántus began to feel that he soon would have finished collecting the flora and fauna of the area. He expressed to Professor Baird his desire to explore Baja California (letter from Xántus to Baird, February 18, 1858, Smithsonian Institution). Baird was not only receptive to the idea, he was eager to have a collection of botanical and zoological specimens from this biologically unknown area examined by his experts. When Xántus's last shipment from Fort Tejon was forwarded in November 1858, Baird obtained an appointment for Xántus as tide observer for the U.S. Coast Survey to be stationed at Cape San Lucas. At the same time, he arranged for Xántus's long-sought discharge from the army. In evident high spirits, Xántus set about his new assignment, as narrated in the following pages.

Ever since coming to California I have had an irresistible desire to see the peninsula of California and travel over the Purple Sea (Gulf of California), both of which are as yet *terra incognita* to the scientific world. Reading the adventure stories of Castelnau* and Edgar Allan

*Count de Castelnau (1812–1880), French explorer, author of *Expédition dans les Parties centrales de l'Amerique du Sud* (1850–59), 14 vols.

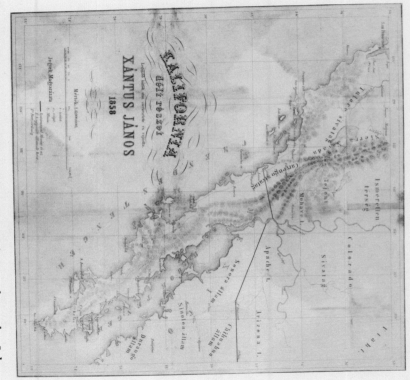

13. *Map of the Southern Parts of California*, drawn by John Xántus, 1858; printed by Haske & Co., Pest, 1859

Poe created in my mind an aura of fantasy of this romantic area whenever my thoughts turned to pearl fishing and other varied adventures that our friend Poe's fertile imagination conjured up.

Only someone who shares my sense of rapt excitement can appreciate how I felt when last spring (1859) suddenly and unexpectedly, this dream of mine not only came true, but under official auspices to boot, and thus I was fortunate to proceed under the protection of a powerful government. A treasury cutter was put at my disposal and the boat was waiting for me at San Diego Harbor, to be boarded with my associates at my convenience.

I received this communication in the evening and immediately started to make my preparations. By six o'clock the next morning I was on my way to my destination, without taking into the slightest consideration that I was facing a journey of more than a thousand miles.

The trip to Los Angeles was of no particular interest, as I followed the same route that I traveled, coming here a year ago. On my way I called on our old acquaintance Mojave Chief Yumusruy-Ekahat-Hum and I was greatly surprised to hear from him that since our last meeting he had embarked on a great journey. He went to San Francisco. Being curious to find out his impressions of San Francisco and the mode of life there, I prevailed upon him to relate his journey in detail. It seems that the horse show performing at the time in San Francisco pleased him the most, for he described the color, the saddle of every horse, and the maneuvers of every rider so vividly that we could almost visualize it. Our friend the chief frankly admitted that it was inconceivable to him how a white man was able to ride a horse with such skill, and his experiences in San Francisco convinced him that the high point of civilization is the art of equitation.

Our Mojave friend was also quite amazed at the large numbers of people living in the city, so far from any hunting ground, and he could not comprehend how they can subsist. He was interested in finding out how many people lived in San Francisco, and so one day he cut a long, rectangular stick, and sat down on the steps of the post office and carved a notch with his knife for every passerby. He continued this operation for hours without stop, to the great amusement of the crowd gathered around him, until at last he realized that the number of the passersby instead of diminishing, was steadily increasing and all four sides of his stick were completely covered with notches. Exasperated, he broke it into pieces and threw it at the young ones around him, although it was his original intention to take it home and show it to his people.

It was an uneventful journey to Los Angeles and from there to San Diego, where after a safe arrival, I had my baggage and animals transported to the cutter, and then looked over the city.

San Diego is the most southern settlement of that part of California that belongs to the United States of America, as the border separating Mexico from the Union is only a few miles from the city. The city was built on a bay of the same name at the northern latitude of 35° 15". The area surrounding the city is a barren desert for hundreds of miles, which cannot support any form of animal life. However there are rich gold, copper, coal, and sulphur mines in the immediate vicinity, but these were not fully developed as yet. The harbor is considered the best on the northern coast of the Pacific Ocean except for San Francisco's, that is between Acapulco and the Fuca Pass, although being open on the east, it is unprotected from the east winds.

The city, outside of the customary four-cornered "plaza" or marketplace, consists of only a few streets, lined with low, one-story, adobe houses, with small windows and flat asphalt roofs. A few churches, and the county courthouse are the main buildings of the city; these, however, are superior neither in size nor taste to the other miserable-looking structures. There is only one printing press in the city, which regularly prints two weeklies, one in Spanish and the other in Spanish and English.

The entire city was built on terrible quicksand, and neither a tree or even a blade of grass is to be seen for miles. The San Diego Mission, which is only a few miles from the city, and which is the only green spot in the entire area, is an exception. Due to the existence of a few deep springs, the Mission enjoys many olive, quince, lemon, orange, and piñon trees. They also grow grapes in limited quantity, which produce a pleasant-tasting wine and the *aguardiente* made from it could compete with any ordinary French cognac. In addition, daily at high tide, a northwesterly wind envelops the entire city in an incredible cloud of dust, so that people are invisible a few inches away. In spite of this, San Diego is healthy and many people assured me that doctors who tried their fortune here soon had to move on lest they starve to death.

The population of San Diego is about 1,500, most of whom make their living by fishing and making salt, while the merchants supply the miners with their necessities.

Towards evening I had put up at an inn, and was pleasantly surprised to meet the proprietor, a Mr. Rainer, a decent Hungarian compatriot who after many vicissitudes wound up in California, and who through the influence of Augustin Haraszthy—who resided at the time in San Diego—was awarded the office of sheriff. Last year, after a stormy election, our friend R. lost his office, but he did not despair. In true American fashion he continued his money-making. He opened an inn and in conjunction with it a blacksmith and horse-renting shop. He is doing very well in as much as his purse is jam full and I am heartily glad of it.

At last, on April 24, after having attended to everything, our cutter raised anchor and, driven by a stiff northwesterly wind, swiftly sailed off. Soon the coastline was left behind in a veil of mist and finally the land vanished from the horizon. While the golden disc of the sun sank in the distant west, to rise again in the east and waken the Hungarian workingman from his dreams, the cutter pitched and heaved over the tall waves under the firm hand of the helmsman.

Anyone who has never sailed the ocean cannot conceive of its awesome beauty, and no description can make him realize the splendor of dawn and sunset on the sea.

I have sailed many times in my life on the ocean and have never tired of it. These are the times that set me free from my hectic activities for peaceful, quiet contemplation. It is pleasant to think of home, country, the loved ones. My passionate soul flies with lightning speed on the wings of fancy to the land of Hungary, where my loved ones greet me with ecstatic joy. . . . But, what if they should not know me, perhaps the absence of ten years has made me unrecognizable; after all, the child that left is a graying man now and the storms that he has encountered have left furrows on his face.

But, no, never.

Maybe the Balaton and the River Drava have become estranged from their old acquaintance, who so often rode the waves in his canoe; it is also possible that the forests and fields where I have spent so many carefree days will no longer recognize an old friend. It may be that my friends, too, have forgotten me, for a white raven is a great rarity in nature, and mutual interests no longer unite us and it is a rule of nature that "the living forget the dead."

But it is not possible that the good soul who rocked me, nursed me, and took care of me, should not recognize me. It cannot be that the one I have rocked so often should have forgotten me, and it is imposs-

93

ible that the one—by now an adult—whom I guided, could become estranged from me. They will know me and love me even if they do not see me for twice ten years, as I know and love them to the end of my days, mother, sister, and brother.

Many of my friends envy my good fortune. But you must not, I beg of you, envy me. For although in my wanderings I have met kind people and many worthy of respect, and oftentimes encountered recognition, sympathy, friendship, even affection, which compensate for life's vicissitudes; while I had the opportunity to behold the great wonders of nature, and observe the antlike industry of a nation with the promise of great power and world domination and prosperity for its citizens, believe me, my friends, the Hungarian can never become American, for his heart and soul can never become as hard as the metal from which the dollar is minted. There is only one place for us in this great wide world: "Home," which may not be great, magnificent or famous, and though poor, is still the most potent magnet for its wandering sons.

The morning of April 28 we sighted land and in a few hours we sailed around Cape Bartolome. At nine o'clock we dropped anchor at Bartolome Bay,* where we intended to come ashore and travel on the western shore of the peninsula to La Paz, and from there return on the eastern shore to Bartolome Bay, where the cutter was to wait for us. I want to mention here that our party consists of twelve people, including two guides and four peons.

Mexico is particularly strict in the examination of foreigners. Their customs and health inspectors always harass the travelers. A passport is indispensable everywhere in the republic. To our great surprise however, we came ashore without anyone inquiring about who we were, where we came from, or where we were going to. This, for us—pleasant—neglect, was undoubtedly due to the revolutionary upheaval in the country.

Bartolome Bay has a spacious and secure harbor, due to the high mountains surrounding it on the north, east, and south. It can only be reached from the west through a channel which is hardly a half mile wide, and which is also perfectly secure, for its average depth is 100 feet.

The bay encloses a small town of the same name, which consists

*Bahia Vizcaino.

of only a few adobe houses and a church, not to mention the numerous miserable huts and caves, in which the wretched, hungry-looking, half-naked population resides. There are a few well-stocked stores in the little town to supply with water, wood, and provisions the many whalers who land in the bay every year.

At the time of our arrival in San Bartolome, they were celebrating some festival; the people gathered from all around the countryside to participate in the procession and the revelry connected with it. There was no end to the huge *carretas* which were filled with women and children or with fowl and all kinds of animals in honor of the *padre*. The *carreta* is nothing but an ox-drawn curricle like that in Somogy, but of far more primitive construction, and the oxen are not hitched side by side but one behind the other. The *paterfamilias* always sits on the shaft from where he prods his team by the unsparing application of a long pole.

As soon as we came ashore, I went to a store to buy some necessities. Hardly was I halfway through with my shopping, when suddenly the shrill sound of raucous music assailed my ears. I stepped into the street where a strange spectacle greeted me. A huge armchair was carried on poles by eight strapping young men, and in it sat an enormous wax figure, more than twice life-size, dressed in overly rich garments, and followed by two *padres* in their full canonic outfits, with lighted, yard-long tallow candles in their hands. Following them were most of our sailors, also carrying long candles, and in their wake, *el popolo* or the *hoi polloi*, singing at the top of their voices, accompanied by the sound of horns, drums, whistles, guitars, and tambourines. Unfortunately, I had just stepped out of the store when the procession reached it so there was no chance of escape. Right then a lighted candle was thrust in my hand by a Mexican with a very serious mien. I immediately thought of my coat, my one and only, which I happened to be wearing, and which was to take my humble self back home to Tejon in a month's time. While I was thus meditating about my coat, the procession stopped without further ado and, in the ensuing confusion, collisions were unavoidable and consequently the flowing wax spilled freely on everyone's neck.

The procession ended in front of the church where a mass was celebrated, after which we were all invited to the padre's home for dinner.

For the evening, an open-air play was planned, but a wind storm

95

blew up which stymied the plan, so everyone got ready for the *fan-dango*, the lively Mexican dance in the padre's hospitable house.

In honor of the guests, *los Americanos*, our Bartolome friends arranged a cotillion which, however, was not successful because this rigid and formal dance is not compatible with the Mexican temperament. The *cuna*, *bolero*, and *italiana* were danced ceaselessly and, after a little practice, I also joined in, to the señoritas' great delight and astonishment that I had learned their national dances so quickly.

Starting the next morning, we traveled southeast. There was a fierce wind blowing throughout our route, which raised clouds of dust, enough to choke one. The area here is barren desert covered with hundreds of different kinds of cacti, among which the most distinct are the *Cereus caespitosa C. Giganteus* and *Cactus opuntia*. Wide spaces are covered with bayonet palms (*Yucca angustifolia*) and in such places it is very difficult to pass, due to the density of the thorns. Jackrabbits (*Lepus callotis*) can be seen by the thousands, and they are so tame that they just sit around, staring at us.

In the afternoon we reached a small village called Zandia where we rested a few hours and fed our animals. We had hardly dismounted when we heard a terrific racket coming from a nearby shed. I looked in to investigate and found a dozen naked lads threshing green stalks of maize with more fierce determination than I had thought a Mexican capable of. The perspiration was pouring down their bodies and into the open troughs before them, there to be mixed with the crushed stalks, which was then boiled in a kettle to mashlike consistency and finally placed in a press which was so primitive that it must have been used in the household of Abraham, the patriarch.

This press was actually a huge, scooped-out tree trunk, covered with a slab of wood hacked flat with an ax. On top of this slab a Y branch was placed, into which a long pole was fitted. Seated on both arms of the pole to exert pressure were women and children, and due to the length of the pole it was seesawing up and down to everybody's great amusement. I suggested improving this magnificent piece of machinery by tying a rope around one end of the pole to a hoop, and transferring the "live pressure" to the other end. "God forbid," responded one of the chaps, who seemed like the general manager, "if I did that, the seesaw would stop, the fun would stop, and I would never get another worker." The chap, unknowingly, was a disciple of Fourier, for he endeavored to make work pleasurable.

Remounting our horses, we continued our journey and the terrain became steadily more fertile and attractive. Near Zandia we saw *Senecio longilobus*, *Martinea proboscidaea*, and wonderful specimens of *Convolvulus*, and further on the *Obione canescens*, *Prosopis glandulosa*, *Riddelia tagetina* and *Abronia mellifera* became quite common as well as many new plants and flowers, as for example the white *Romeria* and several species of *Faluegia*, *Amaranth*, and *Dicteria*.*

Toward evening we reached the village of Cristobal. We settled down for the night near the village as we preferred to sleep in our own clean tents rather than in the adobe hovels of the villagers. The lack of firewood caused us great hardship, as there was none near our camp. We had to gather chamiso bushes for this purpose, and with much effort we gathered just enough to make tea and light our pipes throughout the night, for we were serenaded by the orchestra of a collection of wolves around our camp. They were barking and howling almost without stop, and when they did stop for a second, they started up again with renewed force, much to our astonishment. There were times in my life when such serenading by wolves was amusing, and in no way unpleasant, sometimes however—as at the present time—it chilled body and soul.

In America there are seven entirely different kinds of wolves (*Canis fulvus*, *frustor*, *albus*, *ater*, *griseus*, *nubilus*, and *latrans*) The large wolves can rarely be seen, however, for wherever we went we only met one kind in large numbers, the *Canis latrans* or prairie wolf, which has become quite famous.

The prairie wolf can be found in large numbers in every part of the uninhabited area between the Mississippi and Pacific Ocean, although it is not restricted to this region, for it is just as abundant in Mexico, all the way down to the 21° of northern latitude. Consequently, its name—prairie wolf—is incorrect, if for no other reason than many others of the same species prefer inhabiting the prairies. Whatever questions may be asked about the different kinds of great American wolf, there can be no doubt that the prairie wolf differs completely from all other wolves in the world as to habits and life style. It resembles only the jackal and in fact it is not much different from it, and I would not be too far off if I stated that the prairie wolf is the New World variant of the jackal.

In size it is between the fox and the large wolf; in shape it

*Morning glory, cockscomb, unicorn plant, verbena, mesquite, and other climbing shrubs.

97

resembles the latter, while in sly craftiness it surpasses even the proverbial cunning of the former. The color is gray, sometimes light or dark, depending on the season and climate, but the back is always brown with reddish spots. As to craftiness and cunning, the fox is a mere amateur in comparison. It is impossible to catch the prairie wolf. It was attempted countless times, but the results thoroughly upset the prevailing notion of animal instinct. It would not enter a trap door, but dug underneath it and ate the bait, and disappeared under the door without touching the trap. No matter how well the steel or iron trap is camouflaged, the prairie wolf would not approach nearer than smelling distance, and would contemptuously view the snares from a distance. At night it sneaks into the tents of travelers and steals their provisions. It springs hunters traps with the help of a stone or stick, grabs the bait without being caught, and it is seldom even seen at such times.

The coyote is a constant companion of caravans and traveling parties, which they follow sometimes for hundreds of miles to get at the remnants of food. They lie around the camp, usually beyond shooting distance, although sometimes, when they don't feel threatened by danger, they are not so cautious. Hunters seldom waste powder on them for their skin is worthless. This is why the coyote is especially on its guard when following an immigrant party, sensing that in such company there are always "Sunday" or amateur hunters, who never consider what they are shooting at as long as they can hear the gun go bang, bang.

It follows buffalo herds, too, by the thousands, for hundreds of miles. It usually loiters around the herd, constantly on the lookout for stragglers who fall behind because of illness or because the calving cows are forced to lie down. At such times the whole pack surrounds the unfortunate victim and torments it to death. Sometimes a wounded or old bull may lag behind and will also be attacked, even though the bull will always defend itself and only after a desperate struggle will it succumb, during which time more than one wolf will bite the dust.

Traveling on the prairie one can look for hours and for miles around without seeing a single coyote; should one fire a rifle, however, as if by magic hundreds appear, scurrying around. They rush from their resting and hiding places in order to participate in the prey felled by the gun.

During the night they enliven the camp with their eerie howling, although most travelers could do without such entertainment. Their bark resembles that of a terrier. They always bark three times in a row, quickly, and follow it up with a long and endless howl.

While there is hardly a more cowardly creature on this earth than the coyote, it is savagely cruel. No one is really afraid of it under ordinary circumstances, but there was more than one occasion when entire parties were destroyed by packs of wolves, in raging blizzards, when men were exhausted and the wolves maddened by hunger. But in general, travelers and hunters seldom consider it worthwhile to waste ammunition on them.

We planned to leave early in the morning, but the wolves chased two of our mules and it took us a while to recover them. Finally we got on our way, traversing Cristobal.

Our path was lined everywhere with a dense growth of artemisia and thickly populated with many varieties of rabbit and partridge, this last we saw in covies of many thousands. Here and there we met up with herds of antelope consisting of twenty to twenty-five animals which, as soon as they caught our scent, paused for a minute and then took off with lightning speed.

Around noon we crossed a small creek where we came across many, rare plants like *Cevallia, Aenothera sinuata, Gaura parviflora,* and so on. We also found *Glycyrrhiza,* the root of which is not sweet, unlike the European and Asian variety.*

On the southern slope of the creek we saw for the first time *Larrea mexicana, Fremontia vermicularis, Diotis lanata,* and many other plants. I was very sorry that I could not collect specimens of the infinite variety of cacti, and had to leave this segment of the flora of the California Peninsula to other travelers who are better equipped with transportation facilities then I. I sketched many of them, but hurriedly and without sufficient accuracy to be able to describe and classify them.

The mountains alongside the path were of sandstone, mixed in some places with glistening round quartz gravel and topped almost without exception with thin sheets of basalt.

Toward evening we came upon a large covey of crested partridges, and riding at the tail of the column, I shot seventeen of them with one volley. The California crested patridge is one of the largest and most attractive representatives of the hen family in the world. A fully grown specimen, hen or tom alike weighs about six pounds; the

*Licorice.

99

14. *La Joya on the California Peninsula*, original drawing by John Xántus, 1858;
print by Haske & Co., Pest, 1859

color is shiny ash grey, the wings golden green and deep red with light yellow fluting around the legs. On the head a three-foot and some times a four-and-one-half-foot long black feather rises—just like that of a whooping crane—which it can raise or lay down on the neck. I have seen partridges domesticated in many places on the peninsula, mixing with other domestic fowl and when they hatch their eggs, they remain in the household. I am surprised that these beautiful birds are not as yet acclimated in Europe and I see no reason why they should not multiply there. There are many rich men in Hungary who could easily afford the insignificant expense of transporting the eggs and would it not be a joy to see these beautiful tame birds in our parks?

Late at night, after a ride of fifty miles over seemingly endless melon, cucumber, squash, and pineapple fields, we reached the town of La Joya and pitched our tents in the immediate vicinity.

La Joya, like almost all the other towns and villages of the peninsula, consists of one single building, which is sufficiently typical to warrant a description, so if a town or village is mentioned from now on, unless it is specifically described, the following description would apply.

The structure is of sun-dried adobe, 450 feet in both length and width, being a square, with a courtyard in the center. The building has three stories which are positioned on top of one another in such a way that the top one forms a smaller square than the one below it, thus around each story there is a twenty-five-foot-wide portico formed by the roof of the story below. The walls of the ground floor are fifteen feet thick and all around at a height of twelve feet there are small portholes like windows, but there is no sign of any doors, and only by ladders can one reach the first floor. In the same manner one can climb further up or descend to the chambers on the ground floor on ladders through trap doors. At sundown the ladders are pulled up and the building becomes a veritable fortress to defend against Indians and pirates. This was the reason for this type of architecture.

La Joya has a population of about 800, and here as elsewhere on the peninsula the padre is the leader, being the only educated person. He received us with great kindness and hospitality when we visited him in the morning, and although he had breakfast already, he insisted that we partake of huge amounts of meat which, together with white tortillas flat cakes made of piñon seed or corn flour) and a large pitcher of wine, contributed to our doing justice to his persuasiveness.

I noticed a beautiful mule in front of the building and, learning that it belonged to the padre, I wanted to buy and pay for it in gold, but to my surprise he would not accept gold and demanded *plata blanca*, or silver coins instead. So the deal fell through and we went to visit a church situated in one corner of the building in which a huge wax figure of Saint Dominic above the altar is the outstanding spectacle. The walls were closely hung with oil paintings of the saints, some of them quite good, especially a painting of Saint James with a lengthy inscription from which one learns that the Spanish king, Charles III, presented it to the colony in 1767.

Having explored most of the building, we said good-bye, and once more I brought up the matter of the mule, whereupon his reverence asked to examine my money. Some of the coins were engraved, "5 D" (5 dollars), and others, "Five Dollars." This difference caused no small suspicion on the part of his reverence. At last with great eloquence I explained that "5" and "five" mean the same as the Mexican "5" or "cinco" and "D" and "dollar" are the same as the Mexican "P" or "peso." After listening to my arguments, he looked into my eyes with a serious expression and several times searched the faces of my companions, until he finally agreed that I could pay with the "5 D" pieces, but solemnly protested against the "Five Dollar" ones. Fortunately, I had enough of the former to conclude the sale.

We had hardly left, when the padre called after me to inform me that he had a Papago Indian prisoner whom he would be willing to sell for the "5 D" gold pieces. When I rejected his offer, he burst into a lengthy string of complaints, saying that the Papago Indians rob and destroy the land and pauperize the Christian population, while they, the heathen, are drowning in riches. "*Son muy ricos, tienen muchos caballos, muchos carneras, muchos bueyos, muchos—muchos—muchos,*" gasped the poor padre as we were leaving.

Continuing our journey at long last, we soon left La Joya behind. There was a considerable change in the landscape. Our path led up and down the mountains into narrow valleys. For the most part the surrounding mountains seemed to be composed of amygdaloid sandstone with a layer of chalcedony in some places. In other places huge slag heaps rise to a 45-degree elevation in systematically structured layers. At one place we found an entire hill composed of silicates in one-half-inch thick layers.

The flora is not much different from that encountered yesterday, except for a few tamarind trees and banana palms in the valleys. It is apparent that the area is rich in minerals, if one can judge by the countless number of copper and some silver particles of ore found on the trails.

As I rode a few hundred steps ahead of the company, I noticed on a sandy field, thinly covered with artemisia, a large number of armadillos sitting in front of their holes and growling at me. One of them sitting on its haunches snarled viciously, baring its teeth as if it wanted to stop my advance. It bared its white belly in a challenging way so that momentarily I forgot that I was riding the padre's ex-mule with which I was not yet fully acquainted. Faster than thought, I aimed and fired at the armadillo. But the mule turned around even faster and, after a few desperate leaps, ran swifter than the wind towards the mountains, and just ran and ran until it rushed headlong into a mimosa thicket, which stopped it and it soon calmed down. I rode back to find the place where I shot at the armadillo, but could not find it, and my sense of direction was completely confused.

The armadillo (*Dasypus longicaudatus* De Wied—*D. novemcinctus* Linne) with its bony armor is a very curious animal and is a distinctive phenomenon of the American fauna. Compared to other mammals, the armadillo's skeleton, but especially its skull, is so remarkably different that the naturalist is stirred by wonder. It causes no small problem to museum curators as to its proper placement. The armadillo has no incisors, but is abundantly provided with molars. In the case of one species (*D. gigas*) they number as many as ninety-eight, more than the molars of any land mammal. I have no intention of writing a naturalist's treatise but, to those who would like to know more about the armadillo and cannot come to Mexico, I would recommend Giebel's *Saugetiere*, an excellent work. *

We were late in starting from La Joya and could not complete our planned schedule for the day. At sunset we set up camp near a creek covered with tall, green vegetation and we thought it would have sufficient good water. But soon we found to our regret that the water in the depressions was thickly covered with reeky frog slime. It may have been suitable for the thousands of magpies and crows we roused but it was not fit for human consumption. We had to look for potable water and we finally found some. For supper we roasted some green frogs which we caught in the creek mentioned earlier.

*Christoph G. A. Giebel's book on mammals, published in Leipzig, 1855.

At dawn, just as we were to saddle up, we noticed a cloud of dust on the trail and soon the sound of hoofbeats was clearly audible. Pilka, our Mexican guide, immediately motioned for silence and listened with his ear to the ground. Within seconds he drew his pistol, jumped into saddle shouting, "*Papagos por Dio santissimo, Papagos.*" We all followed his example and in a few minutes the Papago Indians emerged from the dust cloud, but our preparation for battle was superfluous because as soon as the savages rode into our midst, they shook hands and asked us to trade ammunition and knicknacks with them.

Our whole camp was soon transformed into a market place. The Papagos brought beautifully braided shackles, ropes, and whips, also pearl shells, badger quills and parrot feathers. For these we gave in exchange red flannel shirts, a few brass spurs, knives, scissors, sewing needles, and hooks. I traded one of my spayed pack mules for a beautiful young animal. Upon the forceful entreaties of its owner, I threw a red silk handerchief into the bargain.

The men of the Papago band were all of very handsome stature. Many of them wore helmets covered with shiny fish scales and beautiful feathers. The rest of their clothing consisted of panther or lynx skins thrown over their shoulders and deerskin sandals on their feet. Their sight involuntarily brought the ancient Greek warriors to mind.

The easy grace with which they mounted or dismounted their horses (always on the right side), filled us all with admiration. There was a woman among them, too, a cripple whose arms and legs were hardly longer than those of a baby. I could not learn her history, but her face expressed indescribable sadness and melancholy. She sat on a magnificent steed and the obliging and chivalrous manner with which the warriors courted her, and the truly servile willingness with which they strived to fill and even anticipate all her wishes made it hard for me to believe the long list of bloody deeds and plunder attributed to these Indians not only by the padre of La Joya but many others.

Concluding the barter with the Papagos, we shook hands and continued southward, while they went north. In a few hours we reached the Sepada River and a few minutes from there the village of Pulvadera with a population of about 400, and which was surrounded by extensive gardens where greens and fruits were cultivated.

Carrying on further, our path led alongside the riverbank. It soon narrowed between terrifyingly high and steep cliffs, which we had to climb up and down. In one particular place we had to inch our way up an almost perpendicular crag and so we had ample opportunity to observe the capability of the mule. In my opinion a good mule can reach any steep rock that a cat can climb. A square-shaped bundle fell off the back of one of our mules and rolled down the mountain with terrific speed all the way into the valley, the same mountain which the mules climbed without any difficulty.

Artemisia tridentata and *Linosyris dracunculoides* were the only new plants found on our way and in many places in the river we saw thickets of the *Arundo phraguntes* and the *Typha latifolia* entangled. This latter plant, with its broad leaves and purple and milky white flowers, is probably the best representative of its genus. In Hungary they call it "cat tail."*

Our trail, crisscrossed by arroyos or gullies, had narrowed so much by now that we had to climb into the mountains on a side trail to reach an elevation of several thousand feet and, after a further hike of sixteen miles, we managed to get down to the river with much difficulty. To cover this distance took us nine indescribably tiring hours. Our animals were also extremely exhausted. Two of our mules not only dropped but died, and their loads had to be distributed among the other already overloaded animals. According to Pilka—who traveled this route before—this trail is called *el camino del diablo* and I must admit no one could have named it more appropriately than "the devil's highway." The trail seemed endless and its contour resembled a line of rooftops in Holland. Sharp and cutting slivers of basalt and traprock covered it in its entirety. The jingle of the spurs, the thump of the hoofbeats of the mules, the high, black cliffs and peaks, the gaping, shadowy ravines, and the outlandishly shaped cacti with their huge tendrils protruding from among the rocks conjuring up the ears of Mephistopheles—all this almost convinced us that we were traveling towards the underworld. Periodically a mule would drop or die. These we left behind as a sacrificial offering to his Black Majesty.

All our mules were near a state of collapse since they, like ourselves, had not had even a drop of water since the morning. We explored every hollow hoping to find water, but all in vain, there was no sign of it anywhere. As I was searching for water in a hollow formed by slate, I came upon countless number of fragments of a species of huge shells, which possibly belonged to the genus *Innoceramus*, al-

*Sage brush, a tall, reedlike grass.

105

though I cannot state this with any certainty on account of the imperfection of the specimens. At the same place I found many exquisite and transparent examples of rhomboid-shaped limestone.

At last, when we were so thirsty that we could hardly swallow, we reached a high peak from where we could see the much sought water, but in the far distance, in a valley. Our thirst immediately diminished somewhat, and in cheerful mood we descended the twisting trail, joking as if we had been strolling all day toward an Italian resort.

We arrived at the bank of the Sepada where we unpacked our Fahrenheit thermometer; it showed 117° (at five in the afternoon and in the shade) so it was not surprising that we suffered so much. One can only surmise the degree of heat at noon, up on the devil's highway.

That day we pitched camp next to a small village named Socoro, consisting of a single one-story house. The place was surrounded by extensive ruins. In many places red cedar beams were strewn about in an almost perfect state of preservation, which proves that in this climate plant matter will not rot even after centuries, on the contrary it becomes harder and more durable. We searched in vain for objects which would relate to the ancient inhabitants of these ruins. We found no remnants of tools, furniture, or household utensils, except some scattered broken pottery and grindstones for maize, which however are common among all southern Indians. We found so much of this colored pottery, scattered over such a large area, that we began to suspect that they were remnants of waterpipes and not crockery. We also found in the ruins fragments of agate and obsidian, which according to Prescott,* the Aztecs used to cut out the heart of their enemies. One thing is certain: at one time this valley was inhabited by very industrious people, but who they were and what became of them, both Spanish chronicles and Indian folklore fail to relate. It is possible, however, that these ruins are the remnants of more recent times, for in his interesting work of the history of California, Vanegas wrote: "Father Jacobus Sedelmeyer in October 1744 left his mission (Todos Santos) and after an eighty-mile journey reached the Sepada River, where he found 6,000 Papago and the same number Coco Indians"; and on the map in this work the names of numerous Indian settlements can be read, which are still in existence today. Father Sedelmeyer's explora-

---

tions were restricted to the area around the mouth of the Sepada only.

In the morning we crossed the river, left the valley behind, and soon were heading to the southeast amidst rolling hills. In many places we had to wade through knee-deep dust, and for miles there was not even the trace of any plant life. In a few places we passed through tall patches of weeds, but these were also so dry that when a match was put to them they flamed up like gunpowder and in a minute were reduced to ashes. We followed for a long distance a subterranean creek, alongside of which there were many perennial plants in their full foliage, but only a few steps beyond there was nothing green, not even cacti. The aridity was such that it was difficult to realize the rainy season ended only a couple of months ago. The entire region in a radius of about six miles lies considerably below the level of the Sepada and could easily be irrigated, which was undoubtedly done by its ancient inhabitants.

A few miles from today's camp we found more extensive ruins, which were just like the ones of yesterday, excepting for an isolated structure right next to the trail, which resembled some sort of a fort.

Just as we were leaving the ruins, our friend Pilka discovered footprints of peccary (wild boar). Our mules were in such poor condition by this time that we could not follow their trail even if we had wanted to. Our friend St. Vrain, however, left the column and followed the prints to a reedy thicket which seemed to be connected with the ocean. Soon we heard sounds of shots from the thicket, followed by calls for help. We rode over and found our friend in a curious position. His mule, having stumbled on peccaries, retreated in great fright, got entangled in the thicket and fell. St. Vrain was then surrounded by the whole pack which became more and more infuriated after each pistol shot. When we got there, our friend had just fired the last round of his six-shooter and had started to stab the bristly animals with his dagger. The mule was badly lacerated by this time. When the peccary noticed us, they retreated in a pack and then, their bristles raised, rushed at us grunting with unimaginable fury. Each time we shot one, it only increased the fury of the others. Completely disregarding the kicking and trampling of the mules, they were biting and snapping incessantly, until at last, after more than a half hour of this tiring struggle, the last one bit the dust.

The legs of the mules were badly bitten. Both of our dogs were so badly lacerated that we had to carry them in our laps and keep them in the saddle, for they could not walk. St. Vrain's mule was so thoroughly exhausted that we had to load it on one of the pack mules. All this caused us so much misery that we realized we would never reach La Paz without a fresh supply of animals.

European naturalists never fail to brand the American animals as cowardly. Such generalized statement indicates total ignorance. Originally, American animals, when confronted by men, were just as savage as the mightiest animals of the eastern hemisphere, in proportion to the strength and size of the species. The original white settlers in America found the wild animals quite prepared and ready to fight for their territory. But the animals were only accustomed to do battle against the Indians' bow and arrow. Now, however, they had to fight a new and incomprehensible power, a power with such terrifying and miraculous resources, that it filled even the arch enemy, the Indians, with terror. It is no wonder therefore that they, too, were frightened into panic.

The spread of this fear was slow and gradual. The appearance of firearms drove them one after the other to the outskirts of the newly-established settlements before they became aware of the danger. The panther, for example, which formerly attacked man wherever it met him, soon became more cautious, until finally its role changed from attacker to defender. Instead of annihilating him with one quick leap from a tree, it now licks its paws in despair and lets the prey pass by. The black bear, which at one time would have crushed any living creature, regardless who or what it was, presently has become almost a symbol of cleverness. The lynx, which before would ruthlessly tear to pieces anything that fell into its clutches, by now is so accustomed to the smell of gunpowder that it calmly saunters off at its approach.

All these changes cannot be characterized as cowardice, in my opinion, but, rather intelligent accomodation. These animals were confronted with an adversary armed with weapons unfathomable to them and against which they had no defense, so they prudently avoided an encounter, just like any logical thinker who acts according to his experience.

Just the same, I should like to see one of those white, cravatted, and bespectacled scientists from Jena, who trumpet about the cowardice of the American wild animals, come here into the thickets of Mexico and southern California, and attempt to shake hands with the first jaguar or panther he encounters, or give a brotherly hug to a gray bear or make roast pork of a pack of peccary. These scientists would very quickly realize that there are still wild animals left in America, which disregard the number of the enemy, the quality and quantity of their weapons, and which would just as soon make a meal of a legion of scientists as of a mere hamster or mouse.

The fact is that the invention of gunpowder changed the physical, moral, and intellectual face of the world, and changed savage peoples and wild animals as well, and while it roars civilization or war of annihilation into the ears of the savage, it whispers foresight and caution to the wild animal.

Prior to the British occupation of East India, lions, tigers, and other wild beasts committed such daring and extensive devastation that sometimes a single animal destroyed an entire village. Often a large force had to be employed to catch it, and more than once even such a force was put to flight by tigers charging from the bush. When English officers first started hunting lions and tigers it was considered a most dangerous sport, and the papers of the day were filled with bloody and hair-raising stories. In those days tigers were not abashed by red jackets and gold epaulets, but ferociously charged into the hunting party, pouncing on one of the hunters and dragging him into the thicket. What is the situation there today? One no longer hears of cases of a tiger or lion carrying off anyone (except in the northern parts of Bengal, where firearms have not yet penetrated). Tiger hunting on elephantback is so commonplace and so lacking in danger that shopkeepers often engage in it. They stuff their ears with cotton so they will not faint away at the first roar of the tiger.

Today the once feared tiger inhabits only the impenetrable brush and inaccessible caves unless chased from it by rockets, grenades, firebrands, or other instruments of torture, and the majestic lion waits for the attack among rocks and bushes. Unless wounded, it would never initiate the attack.

The fear of firearms is shared not only by wild mammals but also by birds and other creatures, naturally in proportion to their intelligence. Many of my readers know from experience that ducks, geese, cranes, and so on, as well as almost all birds of prey such as kites and crows, are capable of distinguishing between a person approaching armed or unarmed. Their perception is so amazingly accurate that often it is quite difficult to reach these birds.

But as the old proverb says, "there is an exception to every rule," and our lengthy defense of the courage and bravery of the American wild beast is based on this exception. No matter how often other animals might yield to the destructive influence of that dreadful weapon we call the gun, which compensates for man's physical weakness, one thing is certain: the peccary is not afraid of it. On the contrary, the blast of the gun only raises the courage and increases the fury of this remarkable little animal, and it is apparent that what alarms and frightens other animals has no effect on it. Blind, raging fury takes the place of fear in the peccary, although the animal is only eighteen inches high, and barely three feet long.

In natural science classification, I believe the peccary (*Dicotyles* (*Sus*) *torquatus* Cuvier) would be somewhere between the badger and the wild boar. In general appearance it much resembles the badger, while its motley colored bristles which are as long as that of the domestic hog, are very sparse and spiny like that of the porcupine. It has no tail, for the tiny muscular growth cannot be identified as such. Its shoulders, neck, head, thighs, and legs are almost identical with those of the European wild boar, although all these members are thinner, and the nose especially is much more pointed. The peccary lives in packs of ten to forty animals. The tusks are similar to the European wild boar's, which however, are far more formidable due to their peculiar structure, for instead of curling upward they protrude from the jaw in a straight line, and are as sharp as a razor. The animal moves with lightning speed. It is difficult to visualize the terrifying rapidity with which it stabs and pierces with tusks which are only two inches long. The extraordinarily muscular head, neck, and shoulders are a contributing factor. Since peccaries attack everything and everyone without discrimination, whether provoked or not, both man and animal uniformly avoid them whenever possible. Without exception, the entire pack attacks in a unit and the animals fight until the last one drops. It is therefore sheer madness to seek them out and challenge them. There is no animal daring enough to confront and fight them. Men, horses and dogs flee from them with grotesque haste should they encounter them.

We knew all this, and following Pilka's advice none of us went after peccaries except St. Vraint, who could not resist his passion for the hunt and thus risked not only his own skin, but placed our entire party in jeopardy.

Reviewing the battlefield, we took two young piglets of the thirteen two slain peccary and left.

Since morning we have seen many Indian tracks and were in great hopes of meeting them so that we could buy a few horses from them to relieve our mules of some of their burden. Around noon Pilka, who rode ahead, came upon two Indians at a sudden turn of the trail, to the surprise of both parties. Soon we overtook Pilka and our appearance frightened the poor Indians even more, for the only weapons they possessed were bows and arrows, although their horses were good. I do not recall ever seeing more miserable looking creatures; their legs and thighs were shapeless, short and thick; their faces and other parts of their body were completely naked and covered with tiny segments of peeling skin like fish scales. Neither of them spoke Spanish and we communicated by sign language only. We let them know that we wanted to buy horses and mules and that if they would bring the animals to our camp they could expect good trading. One of them talked incessantly, but his speech sounded more like the bark of a sheep dog than a human voice. Both of them just stared, for they were incapable of expressing the joy they must have felt when we left them without harming them or their horses.

Our route took us over diluvial formations covered with coarse, limey sandstone. The mountains around us consisted of red granite, and in the vicinity of our camp dense layers of limestone were visible.

We would have liked to travel as far as Timpa today, but the peccary hunt thwarted our plan, so we stopped halfway near some water holes. We let loose our mules, for the poor beasts were too tired to run away.

Tonight I took on the kitchen assignment, not because I knew much about cooking, but I had complete confidence in my ability to roast a pig. I had a good schooling in this respect in the woods of Somogy, where I saw more than once how the swineherds of Zador go about it.

But to continue my tale. The piglets were hardly on the spit when the alarm "to arms" sounded and, before I could switch from kitchen knives to pistols, the whole company was running breathlessly toward the mules, which the Indians supposedly were driving off; but when we got there we found our animals grazing peacefully, although the entire mountainside was lined with mounted Indians. As we ap-

111

proached them, one called down in pure Spanish, asking for a meeting. "One of you lay down your arms and come here," yelled the same Spanish voice. Manuel—one of our guides—immediately complied and I followed him. We had hardly covered half the distance when the Indian's eyes became riveted on my dagger sheath and, aiming a long-barreled rifle at me, demanded that I lay down the weapon. I threw down the dagger and reached the mountain top where the chief (who was the speaker) received us with barely disguised embarrassment, even though a half-dozen armed Indians were loitering about. The talk was long and boring, during which he told me that he heard from two Indians of the tribe that we needed mules. He said he was prepared to barter with us provided we brought our articles to them to the mountaintop.

All my eloquent attempts to persuade him to come down to our camp proved fruitless. Finally, a handsome young lad laid down his rifle and started to follow Manuel toward our camp, an expression of inexpressible pride on his face. I, too, started to follow, but the chief declared that he would not permit me to leave until his warrior returned safely from our camp. The ice was broken, however, for as soon as the Indians saw that no harm came to their comrade, one by one they all slowly sauntered down to our camp and, after we had traded most of our mules for stronger and fresher ones, we bought three additional ones.

The Indians belonged to the Pinorelo tribe, and there was a middle-aged woman among them whose eternal chatter and constant interference in the bargaining was a veritable nuisance. She wore a red *tulle anglaise* dress, lavishly trimmed with fine quality and expensive Brussels lace, which undoubtedly she acquired from a Mexican beauty going to some sort of a fandango or festival. She sat on a splendid, iron-gray horse, à la Duchess de Berry, and whenever the scarlet cape (alias blanket) slipped off her shoulders, the outline of her figure was clearly visible. After she sold her mule she wanted to sell the horse, too, and constantly made the animal jump and run to demonstrate its noble qualities. Once when she rode up the steep mountainside, the snaps of the back of the dress opened and exposed her entire backside, to the loud and unchivalrous laughter of the entire company. All this did not embarrass our Amazon in the least; she turned back at once and with amazing skill rode down the mountainside. Noticing the problem, she stood up in the saddle and with complete nonchalance pulled the tulle dress over her head, rolled it up, placed it on the saddle and with a quick jump sat on it. Thus, in total nakedness, she rode around our camp for quite awhile, from one campfire to another until she got the prize she was after. St. Vrain presented her with a man's red flannel vest, which she had put on at once, and at last proudly rode off with the salutation, *Adios Señores Caballeros*.

The following day we were in high spirits and made good progress on our new animals. Crossing a mountaintop, we climbed steadily in the direction of the valley of Todos Santos. For hours our path led through a narrow mountain pass, the sides of which were full of tiny iron oxide particles. The composition of the mountaintop was reddish sandstone with layers inclining 25° toward the southwest and under which black slate and dense layers of limestone on a granite base were visible. Tall trees covered the ravines and *Cucumis perennis* in full bloom spread over areas of many acres.

About fifteen miles further down the composition of the mountains changed to gravel and sandstone rubble over layers of red sandstone about 200 feet thick, which were imbedded on a coarse-grained granite base. Most of the sandstone hillocks were covered with thin sheets of vitrous quartz. In a depression we found a green sandstone cave with traces of fire no more than a few days old, the purpose of which we could not even guess.

At ten in the morning we came to the village of Timpa, consisting of a two-story building erected on a mountain slope forming the northwest corner of the valley of Todos Santos, which serves to protect the plantings which are extensive in nearly all parts of the valley. The Indians have small regard for the armament of Timpa, for often they descend from the mountains in large numbers and drive off entire herds of mules and horses right under the nose of the cannons of Timpa.

As we arrived in the village the whole population rushed out to meet and stare at us. I asked one of them if we could get barley or maize for our mules. "*Si Señor Caballero, tengo maize, elote calabazas, melones, y chili tambien, ananas, y papayos,*" was his answer and they brought us ample quantities of corn on the cob, squash, pepper, melons, pineapple, and bunches of bananas. After our shopping was finished, our vendor, who was none other than the *alcalde* or mayor of Timpa, pulled from under his cape a long-necked black bottle and offered it with, "*No quiere whiskey?*" He was much astonished when we told him that we don't drink whiskey, because he heard from the padre that the *americanos* drink whiskey by the barrel instead of water. We asked the *alcalde* if we could see the padre, but he replied that "his reverence" was in Todos Santos, where there was a festival that had already lasted a week, honoring Saint James, and he urged us to hurry if we wanted to partake in the festivities, for they would end in two days.

Alongside the Todos Santos River there is a good *carreta* or wagon trail from Timpa to Todos Santos, but right now the road is flooded in many places because of the rivers overflowing on account of the irrigation of the sugar plantations. Therefore, following the *alcalde's* advice—he was also kind enough to put a guide at our disposal—we chose the mule trail, which led through the mountains at the edge of the valley.

The trail however was far more impassable than we were led to believe, and in order to avoid gaping precipices we had to climb up into the mountains for almost a mile and then down again. Once we had to proceed for miles in the bed of a dry creek amidst steep banks, which greatly resembled the parallel trenches dug by engineers to advance upon a fortress.

As the sun was setting we were still about five leagues from Todos Santos, according to our guide. So we stopped right there in the mountains on the bank of one of the branches of the Todos Santos River.

Both sides of the narrow valley were unusually steep and composed of granite and sandy limestone, with indications of basalt and traprock on the top. On the southern side of the walls where we pitched our tents, tall, yellow, flintlike rocks towered behind us, reaching amazing heights and forming fantastic shapes. One of the peaks was covered with layers hundreds of feet thick, following the direction of the water, and they showed a variation of colors from dark red to pale yellow. The entire mountainside was covered with a powdery yellow, limey sandstone, in amorphoid fragments, presumably under the influence of volcanic fire.

The mountains with their jagged towers and jagged peaks were bare of course, but around our camp there were numerous fan palms, acacia, prosopis, obione, fremontia, chimara, and ephedra growing, but mostly the pitahaya or *"Cereus giganteus"* (one which stood in front of my tent was sixty-four feet high) the world's largest and most

15. *Camping at Night between Timpa and Todos Santos* (California Peninsula), original drawing by John Xántus, 1858; print by Haske & Co., Pest, 1859

unusual cacti with their fork- and column-shaped trunks reaching to the sky, offering such a singular and unique spectacle that we did not regret that the irrigation of rice and sugarcane fields forced us to take this route.

The camp was set up only to await the rise of the moon, so that we could continue with greater ease. Only a few of us lay down, but most of the party sat around a crackling fire and, smoking their pipes, regaled each other with their adventures, as was the custom every night in our camp. Finally, around midnight, a cool wind blew up, so everyone wrapped up in his blanket and soon dozed off in a sitting position. I took a stroll around the camp, reflecting on the many-sided beauty of nature. I stopped at the creek to gaze at the phosphorescence of the huge trunks in which a more timid or superstitious person would see a will-'o-the-wisp or a ghost; then I returned to my companions and dozed off.

Too soon the bugle sounded reveille, however, and in less than a half-hour we were on our way. At sunup we were already in the valley amidst beautiful plantations and gardens, and for miles the wide road was lined with residences, and with palm and orange groves.

At eight in the morning we rode into the plaza of Todos Santos.

Before introducing the reader to the California peninsula's most renowned mission, it is appropriate to describe first the most important plants of this fertile valley, all the more so because they constitute his daily food supply, and he should know how they are grown.

Because of its excellent location, Todos Santos valley seems to unfold all the great varieties of tropical flora. The entire valley is composed of friable volcanic slag and this contributes to plant life, which flourishes all year round and, except on those rare occasions when the Todos Santos River floods over, the plants are bent under the weight of flowers, fruits, ripe and unripe, from January to January.

Cotton has been cultivated in Mexico since time immemorial. Its cultivation and manufacture was well known among the Toltec and Aztec nations. Its adoption for clothing was transmitted from generation to generation, naturally always in proportion to the requirements of the era and the cultural level of the particular generation. At the present time, cotton fabrics are in universal use by all Indian tribes as well as by the descendants of their conquerors. Cotton is planted, although not very extensively, on the slopes circling Todos Santos valley. The local cotton is planted in so-called "black seed" rows, like maize in Hungary, and it grows to a height of four feet, when it bolls sprout and pop, disclosing the content—cotton. A ten- to twelve-year-old child is capable of picking twenty basketfuls a day, the baskets weighing about forty pounds.

Rice and sugarcane are grown very extensively in the valley, wherever the flow of the river can be diverted without too much effort. The yield per acre is far greater than in Louisiana or the Carolinas even though the soil cultivation is not nearly as intensive as in those states. The locally grown white rice is exceptionally heavy and is also planted in rows, although sometimes it, too, is scattered, like barley and oats.

Sugarcane is planted just as it is in Mississippi, Texas, Florida, and Louisiana, with this exception: the plants and rows are much closer together, for they are cultivated by hand and hoe instead of by horse-drawn plough and cultivator. All the hoes are English-made, with pointed blades and long, narrow handles. Sugarcane, like bamboo and maize, is a reedlike plant; it grows twelve to fifteen feet high, and, with its broad leaves and long, silky hair, is a pleasant sight. It's starts to flower nine months after it is planted, then it is cut and put through the various stages of sugar refining, soaking, pressing, boiling, drying, and so on.

In spite of all this, however, the cotton, rice, and sugarcane culture cannot reach its maximum potential either on the peninsula or in any other state of Mexico. This is only possible in slave states where the planter is not subjected to the inconvenience of labor shortages at harvest time, and thus to the risk of the crop rotting in the fields. Although some planters grow a large enough crop to reward their enterprise and industry with not inconsiderable profit, the total production is nonetheless insufficient to fill the peninsula's own needs, and large quantities must be imported annually not only from other Mexican states, but also from Guatemala and Costa Rica.

For the last few years, in some small areas, there have also been coffee plantations in the valley. In the vicinity of the mission, a Scotsman named Ritchie planted 30,000 trees this year, in addition to the 20,000 trees that have been producing for years. Having traveled through coffee plantations before, and therefore being acquainted with planting methods, I think that there are few places on the American continent more eminently suited for the successful production of this important commercial article, than this valley. Yet, not enough care is expended on the planting, cultivation, but especially on the pruning of the trees, although the quality of the coffee is unsurpassed and commands a high price on the local market. On the plantation it costs two reals a pound, and in La Paz almost four reals or the equivalent of one silver florin.

I also saw many cocoa trees in full bloom, especially around the mission, although I have heard that they are not grown as extensively now as before. In comparing them with other trees, they reminded me most of the cherry trees at home both in size and shape. The trunk of the young tree splits into three of four branches. The leaves are about four inches long, smooth but not shiny, and pale green in color, while coffee leaves are dark green. The young tree splits into three of four branches. The leaves are about pleasing sight. The fruit resembles a medium-sized cucumber, but has deep grooves on the sides. The color before ripening is green, which gradually turns to a reddish blue, and finally lemon yellow spotted with pale red. Each pod contains twenty-five to thirty almondlike seeds in a parchment-like cover. As soon as the fruit is ripe, it is picked and sliced, and the seeds, which at this stage are still damp and soft, are dried on palm leaves or on stretched skins. At this point, the cocoa is sour-sweet and can be eaten like any other fruit. The dried seeds are sewn into 100-pound sacks and are ready to be marketed. The cocoa tree grows to a height of about fifteen to twenty feet and, because it does not spread out like other fruit trees, about 400 can be planted to an acre. Each tree brings an annual income of at least four reals, and it is hard to understand why they are not cultivated more intensively, especially since it takes so little effort and also because other plants can be grown in between the rows.

Wherever the eye looks in the length and breadth of the valley one sees the golden tops of the banana and plantain trees heavily laden with the earth's most nutritious fruit, which finds its way to the table of both prince and pauper, civilized or primitive people alike. Its propagation is so simple, just like with the willow tree at home, for all that is needed is to stick a branch into the soil. In about eight months the branch is rooted and starts to spread, and in less than a year after it is planted it is laden with fruit; from then on it blooms continuously and bears fruit throughout the year, year after year. By the time a branch of ripe fruit is cut off, there are numerous young shoots in various stages of bearing fruit around it. Each tree yields about forty pounds of fruit a year, requiring no special care, which makes it easily nature's most valuable gift to mankind.

The banana belongs to the genus *musa* and its botanical name is *Musa sapientium*. It grows in every part of the tropics, its leaves are eight feet long and two feet wide, and its yellow, cucumber-like fruit is six inches long. The ripe fruit is most pleasant tasting and has a prominent place on every table. It is noteworthy that the Mexicans never break a banana in the center but always slice it lengthwise. The explanation given by the padre at Todos Santos was that the inside of a banana resembles a cross, which is the symbol of the sufferings of our Saviour and therefore it is unseemly to split it in half.

The plantain is another precious gift of providence to nourish and sustain the human race under the tropical skies. This tree is also musaceous, and its botanical name is *Musa paradisica*. Its gramineous and soft trunk is about twenty-five feet high, the leaves six feet long and three feet wide. The clusters curling to the top of the tree are sometimes six feet long, and the fruit which soon follows the beautiful flowers alongside the cluster is eight to ten inches long and two inches in diameter. At first it is green, but yellow when ripe, and has an exceptionally fine flavor. The plantain is one of nature's most valuable plants, considering that it is the sole and exclusive source of nourishment for numerous peoples under tropical climes, and its ample yield is unsurpassed by any fruit tree in the world. One cluster ordinarily produces sixty and sometimes even eighty pounds of fruit, and a whole tree may yield 2,000 pounds a year. The fruit of the plantain is edible even in its semiripe stage, but in general it is used when overripe. Sometimes bread is also made out of it, but then it is first cooked and then dried in the sun. The wealthier planters cut it into thin slices, bake it in churned butter and covered with sugar, and serve it as a sweet dessert. Fifty plantains are amply sufficient to feed a person for a week, whether eaten raw or dried, and far more nutritious than wheat bread. Since a cluster can produce 120 to 160 pieces of fruit and an entire tree over 3,000, it is evident that a single tree could feed one person for a whole year, without the addition of any other food.

The pineapple is another valuable produce of this valley, especially because of its exceptionally large size and tangy, zesty flavor. It is grown in large quantities, for it requires no more care than squash or beans. Its propagation consists of merely sticking into the ground the tips of the sharply pointed leaves, and by this method more than 10,000 bushes per acre can be grown. Since its discovery, the pineapple is considered one of the finest fruits in the world, and it is too well known to need further description by me. It is even grown in Hungary in hothouses. In the Todos Santos valley, however, there are many different kinds of pineapple, one of which (*B. penguin*) is grown very extensively and is completely different from the ordinary variety inasmuch as the berries are not bunched together on top like pine cones, but ripen individually and are scattered on top of the spiky leaves. From the leaves of this pineapple fibers are split which are woven into durable clothes or plaited into ropes. The chief purpose of cultivating the pineapple is to make wine of it. The wine thus produced is undrinkably sour for three months, then it turns sweeter and sweeter until, in a few years, it can compete with genuine Malaga.

The mamey and cherimoya, two different varieties of the pomegranate,* also decorate the countryside everywhere. The first is the size of a ten-year-old Hungarian walnut tree, the fruit is about as big and shaped like a goose egg. When ripe, the color is reddish yellow, and it has a brown, hairy, almondlike pit. The taste is tart, however, like that of the quince, and it takes a while to acquire a taste for it. The cherimoya, on the other hand, although a much smaller tree, produces a larger fruit with seeds similar to those of the watermelon and with a pleasant flavor superior to that of the orange. Both trees are smooth and silver-colored, with pale green, narrow, spiky leaves. One hundred of these trees can be planted on an acre, and each one yields an income of at least three dollars a year.

Above all, however, it is the palm that fills the traveler with wonder, for, with its graceful and majestic appearance, it is justifiably the pride of the tropical climes. Its straight, branchless trunk reaching to the sky, crowned with huge and graceful leaves, offers an exceptional and unparalleled sight. But aside from its great beauty, the palm is also practical, for the usefulness of its fruit is the equal of any other plant. The palm belongs to the plants having one cotyledon and a calyx with six segments. The fruit may be like a berry, nut, or apple and consequently may be hard, rubbery, or soft, containing one to three seeds. Among the many kinds, the most important are the coconut, date, and sago palms, and while most members of the species are tall trees, a few grow hardly more than few inches from the ground.

During my stay in the valley of Todos Santos, I was impressed by nature's wise management of its resources: for example, the way a suitable quantity of one species grows on an acre of land without interfering with the sustenance of other plants. Coconut palms, for instance, rise high above coffee, cocoa, plantain, banana, sugarcane, and other plantings without depriving them of nutrition; rather, they protect them from the heat of the burning sun with their parasol-like crowns. Palms planted in this manner need no special care and, if spaced twenty feet apart, ample room remains for the weaker plants to flourish.

The coconut palm or *Cocos nucifera* bears fruit for the first time when it is seven years old, and from then on every tree produces regularly 80 to 100 nuts a year which sell for one-fifth of a real each in La Paz; thus every tree brings a yearly income of three dollars. Coconut palms are grown in the following way: a flat clearing is prepared which is easy to water during the dry season, and the nuts are planted two feet apart in every direction. For two years they are constantly watered and cultivated, after which they are transplanted with great care to their permanent place. The fruit is four to six inches long, eggshaped, the shell filled with thick white, meaty matter. The tree sometimes reaches a height of sixty feet; it has no branches, and the leaves form only at the top, resembling huge green feathers, each of which is at least fourteen feet long and three feet wide. The topmost leaves grow straight upwards, the center ones spread horizontally, while the lower ones hang down. The nuts hang on the top, right under the crown, in clusters of ten to twelve. In the meaty inside of the nuts there is a considerable quantity of sweet, watery liquid, commonly known as coconut milk, which serves as a pleasant, cooling drink in hot climates. The meat of the nut is similar to cabbage stalk, but much sweeter, and it is used in many varieties of food. When pressed, it yields oil—in many places it is the only edible oil—and when it is fresh it tastes like almond oil. The hairy casing of the nut becomes quite flexible if soaked in water for a while, and it is hammered into yarn from which rope is woven, which must be at least as durable as rope made of hemp for warships generally use it. In addition to durability, it also has the advantage of never sinking to the bottom; rather, it floats on the surface due to its elasticity and light weight. The outer shell is so hard that it can be scoured and used as a household utensil, particularly as a drinking cup, sometimes trimmed with gold or silver. The small, tender leaves on the top fold over one another much like cabbage leaves, and are sometimes used in cooking as they are very nourishing

121

and tasty. They are far too expensive, however, if you take into consideration that they would cost the life of the tree. The large leaves of this palm are the sole materials used by the natives for roofing. In addition, they weave baskets, rugs, bags, hammocks, brooms, and many other useful household articles out of them. From the trunk, beams and columns are carved in building houses and boats. When the live tree is tapped, a white, sweetish fluid drips from the wound, which is called "toddy." I have often seen the natives gathering the toddy in large earthenware pitchers, for when it is fresh, it is a much favored drink in the tropics. However, after a few hours it sours and in twenty-four hours it turns into vinegar. The natives make spirits of it by distillation, which is known as "rack" and which is valued higher than rice wine or alcohol made of sugar. When mixed and boiled with lime it turns into honey, which is particularly liked by the natives.

Along the entire valley, but particularly on the seashore around La Paz, I noticed another kind of palm which much resembles the *Sagus rumphii* well known by botanists, although in my opinion it is altogether different. It grows wild in large forestlike areas and provides welcome shade to travelers. The trunk is straight with a widespread, hanging crown of long and lacy leaves. Its edible fruit, no larger than a bird's egg, is covered with a shiny film. In many places the populace collects and presses them in their primitive mills and this is called "palm oil manufacture." This oil is highly valued and is sold at high prices in large quantities in the ports. The trunk contains a flourlike substance from which "sago" is made. This is collected, pounded in mortars, and strained. The sieve is above a trough over which water is poured constantly until all the impurities are removed and the snow-white sago alone remains on the bottom. The sago is then spread in the sun and dried, after which it is put into a drum-shaped sifter for culling. It then looks much like round rice and is taken to the market.

In the gardens of Todos Santos I also saw a few date palms, but nowhere else on the peninsula, although I can see no reason why they could not be propagated. This palm is the most majestic of the entire palm family, for its height exceeds well over sixty feet. The trunk is also straight but covered with overlapping plates which form irregular rings around the waist. The crown consists of twelve-foot long leaves that turn downward and numerous small, overlapping narrow leaves. Male and female are separate in this variety, and the fruit is bunched in twelve to fifteen hanging clusters. The tree is propagated by root division or cuttings. The latter is more practical because shoots of the female palm can be selected and only a few male plants are sufficient for an entire plantation. The young plants require a lot of care and must be constantly watered until they are firmly rooted, and those planted in open spaces must be protected from the heat of the sun by shading them with leaves. Trees grown in this manner bear fruit in six years; otherwise it takes fifteen or even twenty years for this species to reach its flowering and fruiting stage. When the male palm flowers, the pollen is gathered and sprinkled on the female palms. When the fruit is ripe, the clusters are cut and hung in a dry place for the liquid to evaporate, thus making it suitable for packing. There is no need to describe the fruit, for everyone is familiar with it, except to note that in its fresh stage it has incomparably better taste and flavor than those available in the stores. All the same, the dates in the store are not processed in any way, but remain in their natural state as picked from the trees. A cluster of dates which normally weighs twenty to twenty-five pounds sells for five to six reals in La Paz, where, however, it is a rarity.

The date palm not only produces a delightful fruit, but is also utilized for many other practical purposes, for from its very roots to its highest leaves every part is serviceable. The tree itself is hard and provides an exceptionally durable wood for building purposes. The leaves after soaking become very flexible, and hats and baskets are woven of them. From the fibres of the inner bark very strong and durable rope is made. In addition to all this, palm wine is made from the trunk in the following manner: the leaves are removed and the trunk under the crown is cut in a half circle, and then another vertical cut is made, under which a receptacle is placed to collect the sap. The collected liquid is then boiled. The product is a pleasantly refreshing drink, which is however too sweet to be called wine. Sometimes brandy is also made out of the fruit, and a good quality oil is pressed from the crushed seeds.

Outside of palms and other useful plants, there are also fig, olive, orange, lemon, and tamarind trees in the valley, but I intend to describe these in detail at another time. Right now I shall continue the interrupted story of my journey.

Todos Santos was founded by the Jesuits at the beginning of the last century on the banks of the river and in the valley of the same name. At present it is a flourishing little town, although its most important building is still the mission which consists of a magnificent church, cloister, and auxiliary buildings enclosed in a huge, walled square.

As I mentioned before, the mission was founded by the Jesuits, who were the first to colonize the peninsula. The missionaries sent here were invested with unlimited power by the Mexican church authorities. They were the sole and absolute rulers of the land. With their well-known indefatigable industry and boundless energy they applied themselves to everything to promote the welfare of the church and the advancement of religion. They built factories, planted gardens and plantations for their own comfort and that of their converted flock. They built huge cloisters and churches to worship God according to the rituals of their religion.

In this century who would think of building a church and cloister in the utter wilderness that resemble a magnificent fortress or castle, occupying about fifty acres of land? And who would build walls 15 feet thick and 100 feet high? All this was accomplished by the Jesuits without the help of expert craftsmen, guided only by their religious fervor. They spread the Christian faith everywhere, converted the savages, and without using force, brought them down from their mountains and forests to build churches for the glory of God and their religion.

The building of the mission took twenty-five years of unrelenting work. At times 5,000 Indians worked on them. Most of the buildings were constructed of sun-dried adobe, but the church itself is of carved stone, as are the foundations, vaults, and columns of the other buildings.

After the banishment of the Jesuits in 1836, Franciscan friars took over the mission, and as of today they are in undisturbed possession of it, although at present it is occupied only by one padre and two chaplains. Padre Juan Molina received us with the world-renowned hospitality of his order and obligingly offered to guide us to inspect all the worthwhile objects in his mission. Having already described the missions at San Gabriel and San Fernando, all I can say at this point is that, with very few exceptions, they are like this one.

The altar area of the church is under a 125-foot high cupola, which gives the building an appearance of splendor, both in and out. Although there are signs of decay, the interior is truly very beautiful. The spectator is moved to reverence, visualizing its former pomp and glory. The main altar is lovely and is in the best of taste. It is very simple, yet it inspires deep religious feeling. It is this very unpretentious simplicity which evokes thoughts of a higher sphere, so that all earthly ideas turn toward the greatness and majesty of the divinity.

As to the festival, we were misinformed by our friends in Timpa. It was not in honor of Saint James, although he was incidental to it. The real purpose of the festival was to commemorate the laying of the foundation stone of the mission, which took place on May 1, 1974, and which happened to be the anniversary of St. James's birthday. The populace that was to participate in the festivities gathered at the plaza surrounding the mission the day before the start of the festival, and the scene resembled an army camp more than a religious gathering. But the festival lasts an entire week and the daily ceremonies are just repetitions of those of the first day. They open at sunup with the firing of cannons, after which the padre celebrates high Mass in the church and one of his assistants preaches a sermon. After lunch there are bull and bear fights, sometimes horse and foot races, cock fights, and so on, and finally a fandango ends the activities for the day. The dancing never stops before the crack of dawn.

The foot race is no small achievement and the audience follows its course with feverish excitement. The racecourse is ten miles long, and the runners are obliged to propel a wooden hoop with the right foot only, up to the finish line.

As at all such gatherings, a large amount of wine and other alcoholic beverages is naturally consumed, and on account of this countless amusing incidents occur. On this occasion, for example, an inebriated citizen was leaning on the rail of the plaza lost to the world, when a bull, fleeing from its tormentors, jumped out of the bullring and dug its horn into the seat of the pants of our surprised citizen, hurling him up and dropping him in the dirt in a froglike position. The audience naturally roared with laughter at the unexpected entertainment and the citizen not only sobered up in a hurry but assumed a ghostlike appearance, as though he had just been given his last rites. But no real harm came to him, except for the rip in his pants in memory of the festival of St. James.

Another lad, stimulated by having emptied a couple of bottles of *aguardiente*, evidently imagined himself the bravest of the brave, and jumped on his mount, a spear in his fist and without any ceremony tore after the bull. However, his greeting was immediately and appropriately reciprocated so that horse and horseman hit the dust simultaneously and it was a miracle that both of them did not give up the

ghost. The effect of this incident on our swaggering and proud caballero was not only amusing but almost miraculous, for there was no
more sober person in the entire assembly after this.

Many pretty women participated in the fandango that evening.
They were all dressed in the latest style, in full skirts. The dancing
continued without any mishap, the ladies were friendly, beautiful, and
enchanting, the music was tolerable, and the food and cooling drinks
left nothing to be desired. It seemed to us that everyone had a good
time, and what pleased us most was that everybody went out of his way
to entertain us so that we should not easily forget the St. James festival.

During the festivities we made the acquaintance of a wealthy
merchant from La Paz, who introduced us to his wife and two charming
daughters. We were much surprised that Mr. Sepulveda's Christian
names were "Jesus Maria Christopher," his wife's, "Jesus Maria
Catalina," the older daughter's, "Jesus Maria Gabriela," and the
younger one's, "Jesus Maria Juanita. According to Spanish-American
custom when ladies are addressed, the full given names and the sur-
name must be mentioned; for example, if one takes leave of several
ladies, instead of the European, "Ladies," one must address them
individually with their full names and surnames. It is easy tó imagine
how strange it sounds when, conforming to the custom, we say: "*Adios,
Señora Jesus Maria Catalina Sepulveda; Buenos suenos, Senorita Jesus
Maria Gabriela; Buenos suenos, Senorita Jesus Maria Juanita; Adios,
Donnas Senoras.*"

The capital of the peninsula, La Paz, is only a few miles from the
mission, although the winding river road makes the distance unneces-
sarily longer. The road, however, is good and in many of the level
places paved; the gullies, ditches, and streams are bridged everywhere
with such durable material that the highway is the equal of any European one.

We left the mission accompanied by a large number of people,
since many citizens of La Paz joined us as we returned home from the
festival. The padre of Timpa, with whom incidentally we became great
friends, also decided on an excursion to the capital in order to show us
personally the "elephants."

The padre of Timpa was a very amusing man, and our initial
contact was very characteristic. After asking our names and occupations, he learned that we were connected with the American engineer-

ing corps, whereupon he immediately remarked: "Ah, then you know astronomy and geometry?" "A little," was our answer. The padre then took his portfolio and sketched many objects on a page while turning to us often and asking:

"Estes es el cuadro?"
"Yes, it is a square!"
"Este un cerco?"
"Of course, it is a circle!"
"Y este es un triangulo?"
"Undoubtedly it is a triangle!"

Apparently quite satisfied with the result of his questioning, he hid the portfolio in his voluminous stole, rubbed his hands, and said with a smile: *"Ah! voy que vino son astronomos y mathematicos grand- os!"* And so the padre of Timpa solemnly declared that he was convinced that we were great astronomers and mathematicians, and as a result he would not leave our company for days, and whenever he met any acquaintance he would not miss introducing us with an air of great self-importance: *"Estos caballeros–mios amigos–son grandissimos astronomos y mathematicos Americanos!"*

There was lively traffic on the highway and signs of civilization cropped up everywhere. Both sides of the road were edged with gardens and plantations, and, amid the bamboo and coconut huts, tasteful and charming villas peeped through, which were very attractive with their flat roofs and wide verandas. The entire highway was full of squeeking *carretas*, mules and donkeys, some going to the valley empty, others going to the market in La Paz, loaded with produce, gold, and silver.

We were much amused by the laconic answers we received to our questions from some of the people we encountered on our way. The questions and answers were, for example: "Where are you coming from?" *"De abajo"* (from down there). "Where are you going?" *"Arriba"* (up there). "What's the news?" *"Nada"* (nothing).

People who are capable of giving such firm yet indecisive answers are undoubtedly endowed with wit, for I think that there is more wit in these answers than, for example, in the standard Mexican joke: *"Comprendo pero no quiero"* which is so foolishly applied all over the republic.

All the same, the inhabitants of the peninsula are not as taciturn

127

and cold towards their countrymen. On the contrary, they are polite and loquacious. When they meet there is no end to the hugging and kissing, and inquiries about the welfare of every member of the family, and finally, after a lot of handshaking, they pray that everyone will be blessed by the protection of all the saints. I don't want to omit mentioning one particular form of greeting which I heard from the lips of one of the mule skinners on the California peninsula. When we met him, the padre recognized him and greeted him with the customary, *"Hola muchacho mio—viva usted mil años!"* to which the mule driver took off his hat and answered as follows: "May God and all his saints keep you in good health, dear Reverend, so that you may be present at the celebration of my 1,000th birthday!"

In the evening of May 7 we arrived at La Paz, the capital of the peninsula and the seat of the government and bishopric. Its population is not yet 10,000 but it is steadily growing for its harbor is the best and safest in the entire Purple Sea. With the exception of the harbors of Constantinople and New York, there is hardly another in the world that can accommodate as many ships as the one at La Paz.

The town is at 24°08′ northern latitude and 110°10′ western longitude (the same latitude as southern Egypt and middle Arabia—Mecca), surrounded by such lush tropical vegetation that a more picturesque and attractive landscape is hard to visualize. The harbor at the mouth of the already mentioned fertile Todos Santos valley is also the center of the richest pearl, sponge, and coral fishery. In addition, there are many productive mines in the immediate vicinity of the town. It requires no prophet to state with certainty that in a few years La Paz will be one of the most important cities on the shores of the Pacific Ocean.

Such a change can only come about at a snail's pace, as long as the peninsula belongs to the Mexican Republic, for flourishing commerce in Mexico is unimaginable. For example, import and export duties vary from port to port and constantly change with the change of governments. It happens many times that ships arrive at the harbor, but because the governor of the peninsula has raised the duties the day before, they do not drop anchor but seek out a cheaper port to unload at, or else cruise up and down while their agents bribe the governor to reduce the duty. It often happens that, being unable to achieve their goal in this way, any number of English and French vessels will sail to

Valparaíso or even to the Sandwich Islands to wait there until the Mexican government should fall and a new government take office. As the reader knows, for the past quarter of a century Mexico has been in a state of permanent revolution. Often three presidents are banished in a single year or (as at present) three of them rule at the same time.

If, on the other hand, the peninsula should become the property of the North American Union, which is only a matter of time, for it will inevitably happen before long, then La Paz will become one of the main depositories of American industry; every product intended for Mexican consumption can safely be stored here until advantageously marketed and in sufficient quantities to meet demands. Furthermore, due to its geographical location, La Paz could become for the North American Union what, for example, St. Helena, Gibraltar, Malta, or Bermuda constitute in the hands of the British—the protective shield for all American whalers and commercial shipping scattered in the South Pacific in case of a war with any of the maritime powers. Moreover, La Paz could serve as a distribution and communication center for American steamship companies, where they could replenish their supplies on their own territory, instead of (as at present) being forced to do so in foreign ports at uncertain tariffs. Foreign shipping would also have access to the port at any time, for the tariff would be set by the Congress in Washington and would therefore be permanent and uniform so that shippers in London or Le Havre could calculate the cost in advance.

For the aforementioned reasons, at the present time La Paz's foreign trade is very limited. Currently its commerce is restricted to ports on the other shore of the Purple Sea, and nine-tenths of all produce, ores, and pearls are shipped to Mazatlan and Guaymas, whence they are forwarded on muleback to Vera Cruz or Mexico City and then distributed to all parts of the world at excessive costs. English, French and American manufactures get here by the same route, instead of by direct sea route, which could be just as cheap here as in London, Paris, or New York. An ordinary Sheffield knife or fork would not cost one dollar, which is almost the equivalent of a silver one in La Paz.

As soon as we arrived in town, we dismounted and I sent my letters of recommendation to the appropriate authorities, to plan a program with them that would include everything noteworthy in the town and its vicinity. I believe such procedure is practical, especially

129

when there is only a limited time at one's disposal and there is a chance of missing the most important sights by aimless wandering. Long experience has taught me that when a traveler arrives in a foreign city, it is best to plan a daily schedule from which there should be no deviation except for a physical cause, and even in that case one should eliminate the least interesting items lest, as the old saying goes, "He went to Rome without seeing the Pope." Years ago in New York I had the pleasure of meeting two Hungarian travelers. One of them was interested in mining, and the goal of the other was to study the relationship between free and slave labor. Two months later I happened to meet them again in St. Louis and they were discussing at length the theatre in New York and Philadelphia, and the beauty of Niagara Falls; but when I asked for their opinion of the mines in Pennsylvania and the plantations in Virginia and Maryland, they were forced to confess that they had not had time to look into them. When I offered to give them letters of recommendation to some planters in Louisiana and Tennessee, and also to gold mines in Georgia and the Carolinas, they turned it down because a certain Mr. Bernstein had provided them with statistical data, and also they were going to return to Hungary in a few weeks. I do not know whether my compatriots published their American findings. If they did, I am sure the knowledge of economics and of mining gained much through the important statistics provided by Mr. Bernstein—an eccentric German Jew (who was also a brewer and editor of a journal), who at that time had lived in the country for one year, and who knew as much about conditions in America as the shepherd of Tarnoca about the structure of the electric telegraph.*

The French consul, Mr. Rochambeau, came over in person as soon as he received our letters of recommendation, and in his company we hastened to the house of Mr. Watkins, the American consul, where we soon felt quite at home. Following the kind and expert advice of our new friends, we decided to keep a strict schedule for the short period we were to be here. We examined every notable building and institution in town; we made excursions to the nearby islands to learn about pearl, coral, and sponge fishing; we visited a few gold, silver, and sulphur mines; nor did we neglect our collection of naturalia, yet we

---

*Tarnoca is a small village in Hungary. Xántus is being sarcastic; the shepherd of Tarnoca means an ignorant country yokel.

had time to go to the theatre in the evening, to dance a few boleros in the fandango, and to acquaint ourselves with the characteristics of family and domestic life in the region. We could do all this only by conscientiously sticking to plans.

One of our excursions was to Cape Pichalinqui where the steep underwater shores are literally covered with pearl shells, and the sandy bottom of the straits between this cape and Cerralvo Island is heavily encrusted with a coral forest that stretches for miles. The bay and the cape, as well as the submerged coasts of the islands in the bay, are blanketed with an enormous bank of sponges.

All these important commodities concentrated in one place naturally caused considerable excitement among adventurers who, in the hope of gaining a fortune, were willing at the risk of their lives to brave the depths of the ocean and bring the hidden treasures to the light of day.

Fishing for coral and sponge, but especially for pearls, dates back to the discovery of the Purple Sea and was always pursued with great industry and much competition, particularly from the middle of the last century to the beginning of this one. One cannot even estimate the value of the pearls fished so far, but the reader can try, knowing that at times as many as 200 boats fish at the same time and some of them leave with no less than $200,000 worth of pearls; there are no instances of a boat ever leaving with less than $40,000 to $50,000 worth of pearls. At the present time, on account of the unstable internal conditions in Mexico, fishing has declined considerably, but even so, while I was here there were more than ninety-six boats around, employing about 1,500 divers.

Unlike divers in the East Indies and Persia, they do not dive here with bells because the razor sharp coral cannot be approached in glass bells.* Only Indians and halfbreeds are employed. Relying not only on their swimming ability but even more on the capacity of their lungs, they dive straight down to a depth of forty to fifty feet from a plank extending from the side of the boat, and reach for the shells among the coral branches. The divers are completely naked. Their sole equipment consists of a wire basket attached to their belt and a double-edged knife tied to their arm. With the help of the latter they strip away the

*In the East Indies the pearl diver descends in a glass bell.

131

shell from the coral reef, put it in the basket, and just as they are about to suffocate, with lightning speed they surface, gulp air for a few seconds, and immediately dive down again.

In this way, a good diver can fish for half a day, sometimes even an entire day, without stopping, seldom using more than five minutes, ordinarily not more than three, for breathing. With each dive he brings up two to three shells, which he throws into a basket or pail lowered from the boat. It happens sometimes, however, that he does not bring up anything; at other times, as when we were present, he brought up five shells and ten small size pearls in a single dive.

The mollusk which produces the pearl lives in a double shell six inches long and four inches wide, the interior of which is lined with a shiny glaze of many colors and which is known as mother-of-pearl and used all over the world on penknives, shirt buttons, cane knobs, and all kinds of luxury articles. The exterior of the shell is made of a dirty pinkish material, coarsely grooved, which is anything but pretty. The sides of both valves are of evenly structured layers of spaces which are receptacles for the pearl. These are hermetically sealed while the pearl is attached, but once the pearl is removed, holes develop in the shell as a consequence of which the oyster soon perishes.

There is a widespread belief that the pearl is the result of a diseased oyster. It is no wonder that people believe this when even some naturalists of high standing are of the same opinion. All the same, this opinion is wrong, for the mollusk is in perfect health while the pearls are in the shell and becomes sick only when the pearls start to fall out. A few days later, it dies. The cause is natural and simple. In the places where the pearls fall out, holes develop through which the water penetrates and the mollusk, unable to seal itself airtight—which is indispensable for its survival—perishes.

A perfect shell ordinarily has twelve pearls of which the lower ones are the largest, and they gradually diminish in size until the uppermost ones are no larger than a pinhead. As a result, pearl fishers and merchants designate pearl sizes by numbers. The numbers are quite similar to the size of shots. The largest is the size of a musket ball and carries the size of 00, the next size is 0, followed by pearls of rabbit shot size, all the way to bird shot size, numbering 1 to 10. Assuming the quality is equal, the value of the pearl depends on its size, and since live shells are rarely found, and the pearls fall out of the live

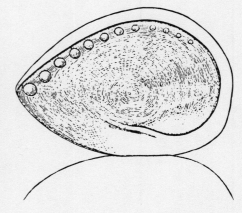

16. *Interior of La Paz Pearl Shell* (one-third actual size)

Interior of La Paz pearl shell.
About ⅓ of original size.

shells, most of the shells brought up are empty, or contain but few pearls, and in consequence the large pearls are rare and expensive.

Locally the price of pearls varies considerably. During our stay here it was as follows:

#00	each pearl	20 reals
#0	each pearl	12 reals
#1	each pearl	8 reals
#2	each pearl	6 reals
#3	each pearl	4 reals
#4	each pearl	2 reals
#5	each pearl	1 real
#6 to #10	per lot	30 reals

One can buy them much cheaper, however, from independent Indian fishermen, especially in exchange for silk stuff, penknives, and so on. For example, I traded four silk handkerchiefs for a sackful of pearls, all told 115 pieces of various size (about fifty dollars worth for three dollars), and some members of our party have done even better.

Most of the divers and boat owners are completely under the thumb of a few rich pearl merchants, however, and it is very difficult

133

for a stranger to buy pearls firsthand. The poverty-stricken populace are the helpless tools of the fisheries and, in their eternal need, turn to the merchants who never refuse to let them buy goods on credit at highly inflated prices. Moreover, the divers drink and gamble, are always short of money and never out of debt. Mexican laws entitle the creditor to force the debtor to work off his debt, and thus most of the divers are virtually enslaved, for it is in the interest of the merchants that the debtor should not be able to pay off his debt. The pearl merchants are therefore constantly keeping an eye on the divers, and very seldom can an outsider get a pearl from them.

After the pearls are removed from the shells, they are put in numbered boxes corresponding to their size; the shells are also collected in different baskets, depending on their quality, because the shells are as valuable commercially as the pearls because of the mother-of-pearl. About two million pounds are shipped annually from La Paz, where at present the price is 32 reals per 100 pounds.

I must not forget to mention that the life of the diver is endangered not only by the hazard of drowning, but is constantly threatened by a far more terrible menace. The habitat of the pearl oyster happens to be the favorite hunting and fishing ground of sharks, and the countless variety of fish, mollusk, and crabs in the coral reefs constitute the shark's favorite food. It often happens that a shark attacks a diver. If it does not kill him outright, it takes off with a leg or an arm. Such tragedies are daily events. Sometimes, after a desperate struggle, one or the other wins, and at such times it is mostly the diver who prevails because, having seen the approaching shark in time, he can easily slit its throat with his double-edged knife, as the monster turns on its side. Nature in its wisdom has put the mouth of the shark not on its head, like other beasts of prey, but on its underside, so that before it can devour its victim it has to turn on its side to be able to bite and swallow with its serrated mouth. According to the statistics of the last ten years, sharks devour 3 percent of the divers of La Paz every year and maim about 15 percent.

At the present time coral is not being fished to the extent it was years ago when it was still believed that it had some medicinal value, and preparations were made of it in various forms like powder, mixture, resin, and so on, and used for the prevention of many diseases. Today, however, it is generally recognized by the medical world that coral has no more healing power than any other oyster shell or the shells of any other animal composed of calcium carbonate. Furthermore, recently extensive coral islands were discovered in the South Pacific, which are as nice and as good quality as in the Purple Sea, and are far more accessible.

To date coral has been used only for jewelry. While coral of good quality is found closer to home, in some parts of the Mediterranean, I think it may be of interest to the reader to know that every natural scientist accepts for a fact that coral is a living animal. It grows as a rule on the sandy bottom of the sea, although sometimes it can be found on the coast as well, as for example here at the Purple Sea. In shape it resembles a bush deprived of its leaves, or a dwarf tree with numerous branches. The trunk is about two to three inches in diameter with a base twice this size, which enables it to adhere to the sand. The entire bushlike animal is covered with a gray, velvety, mucous matter which is actually the living part of the animal (the coral bush is really the shell housing numerous cohabiting polyp-like tiny animals). After the coral is fished out, this matter is removed by rubbing it with coarse brushes and the branches are polished smooth with coarse sand. The inside of the branches is extremely hard, of many colors, from milky white to dark red, and can stand the most abrasive grinding and polishing. Coral in its natural state is marked with lines from end to end and the exterior is layered with tiny plates which are easily dissolved by heating, so that the entire matter becomes a solid colored, heavy and dense body. The chief chemical ingredient of coral is calcium carbonate colored with iron oxide, mixed with animal matter just as is the case for all calciferous growth. In La Paz at the present time very little is fished, because there is more piled up at the market than there is a demand for, in spite of the low price of 20 reals per 100 pounds. The fishing is done in the following manner: equipped with a half-dozen wire cords, the diver dives to the bottom, fastens the hooklike ends of the cords to the coral stems, and after securing as many as he can, surfaces. The other end of the cord is attached to a cork float which of course stays on the surface of the water. In this way, the coral is broken off and pulled up to the surface. If, however, a complete specimen is wanted for a collection or for scientific purposes, the diver equips himself with a small axe and hacks out the specimen by the root and secures it by hooking it above its base. I saw such a specimen in Mr. Rochambeau's house. It was intended for the botanical gardens in Paris. It was nine feet high, weighed 174 pounds, and its coloring resembled red marble with blue, white, and gray veins.

The sponge is also one of nature's wonders which, until recently, was considered to be a plant, but today the scientific world accepts as indisputable fact that it is a live, flexible, rooted, and multiformed animal which, depending on its many varieties, consists of partly oblong fibers and partly tiny, artificially entwined pointed or flat platelets. The entire tissue is covered with slimy fleshlike matter which contain countless tiny openings to ingest and digest water, or to squirt out an excess of it. The sponge family is found over a widespread area but to date the finest textured species, mostly used in Europe, come from Greece and the Red Sea (*Spongia officinalis*). About seventeen different kinds of sponge are fished around La Paz, but none of them are suitable for medical use for they are too coarse. Nevertheless they are an important commercial commodity, for while they are not fine, they are rather large. I have seen many samples myself, each of which weighed not less than twenty pounds. These sell for a good price for they are used to clean the decks of ships. At present La Paz sponges sell for 15 to 20 reals per 100 pounds.

Sponge grows invariably in a depth of thirty-nine to forty feet and is always attached to rocks, coral reefs, or other hard matter and, as he does for pearl shells, the diver severs them with his knife. Brought to the surface, the mucous flesh is rubbed off with coarse sand, then it is soaked for days until it finally dried out. Then it is softened with a wooden mallet, washed once again, and is now ready for the market. At this stage, however, the sponge is not yet quite clean. The pores are still filled with gravel, coral, and tiny shell fragments, which of course have to be removed before the sponge is ready for general use. There are many sponge cleaning establishments in La Paz. The process is as follows: The sponge is soaked for several days and softened in cylinders and the remaining shell or other remnants dissolved in hydrochloric acid.

An indication of the peninsula's wealth in precious metals is the presence of 215 gold and 160 silver mines, although not more than one-eighth of them are in operation at the present time. Owing to lack of capital and internal instability, the rest of them have been abandoned, many of them collapsed, and some of them are flooded. There are many mines in the vicinity of La Paz which are operated negligently and inefficiently on account of a lack of enterprising spirit and capital. The local silver has no special merit, it is always intermixed with other ores. Smelted down, it contains 26.4 percent pure silver (the silver ore in Transylvania yields 35.4 percent pure silver and only the one from Sinarowsky is purer than that, according to Dufresnoy).* Gold however is found in various forms.

In many places here this noble metal turns up in eight- to twelve-sided, symmetrical crystals of various sizes, particularly in dry rivulets and mountain streams. Sometimes, however, gold appears in irregular shapes from lentil or pea size to chunks as big as a fist, and there are instances when a piece weighing 100 pounds has been found. Pieces no smaller than a pea and as large as a walnut, are called *pepita*, and larger pieces are called *pedazo*. When the gold is smaller than a pea but is round and not flat it is called *polvo*, while the small fish-scale shaped piece is called *lantejuela*. All these different shaped pieces of gold are found scattered over water and dry land, mountains and valleys, and all that is required is to search for them, collect and sell them or, if they are very small and mixed with sand or soil, to pan them.

In the gold mines, however, the metal always appears in quartz lodes or veins, and its extraction is accomplished by systematically organized mining methods. In its natural state, gold appears either in very fine, gossamer, spider weblike leaf-shaped flakes, or in very narrow veins formed by tiny granules and crystals. But most of the time it appears in small particles, hardly visible to the naked eye; it is then broken into tiny fragments, ground, and smelted.

The local gold ore is of high grade, for it averages 89.58 percent pure gold, which about equals the famous ore of the Miaski mines of Siberia, but the gold content is far greater than in the ores of Hungary and Transylvania. (According to Dufresnoy, Hungarian ore contains 60.50 percent and Transylvanian 64.52 percent pure gold.) One wonders why these mines are not worked more efficiently and with greater precision.

In order to give the reader an idea about mining operations here, I will relate an experience. When we reached Algua, a nearby village, Mr. Rodgers, an Englishman who operated several mines in the vicinity, joined us and was kind enough to offer his service as a guide. Climbing the mountain, we found both sides virtually covered with

*Petit Dufresnoy (1792–1857), French geologist.

holes dug up by prospectors for gold. In fact the entire mountain as far as the eye could see was dug up in this manner. Here and there we saw a number of miserable-looking men in rags or even naked, digging with primitive iron bars while others were gathering the dug-up soil into goat horns and washing it in the stream. They worked all day at this, and in the evening they took the collected gold dust into town where they spent it gambling and drinking.

Soon we arrived at Mr. Rodgers's mine headquarters where he had erected three mills, two of which had fallen apart months earlier and, since he was unable to get anyone capable of reconstructing them, only one was in operation at the moment. It is difficult to imagine a simpler machinery than this mill. The entire thing consists of a circle twelve feet in diameter and one foot deep, the bottom of which is lined with heavy, flat stones. There is a vertical shaft placed in the center of the circle from which three horizontal beams extend. A pair of oxen are yoked to the longest beam and huge stones are fastened with ropes to the other two which, when started by the oxen, pound the circle round and round with a terrific clatter.

The quartz thus broken into small pieces is put into the circle and a few pailfuls of water are poured over it. Then the oxen start their monotonous plodding and carry on until the quartz and water turn into mud within the circle. Then a few ounces of mercury are scattered into it, the pounding is resumed, and a short time later the mud is thrown off and the mercury-gold amalgam is collected from the bottom, put into leather pouches, which are then placed into earthenware pots, and the mercury removed by smelting.

Scattered around the mill we saw iron ore of exceptional purity which is mined everywhere together with gold. Mr. Rodgers was very generous and offered us as many gold quartz and iron ore pieces as we could carry, leaving the selection of the samples to us.

From the mills we went to the mines, which are actually wide and deep shafts, and into which one descends on rungs cut into poles. From the bottom of the shaft tunnels lead into the bowels of the mountain, where miners blast out the quartz with gunpowder and pickaxes. This is done without any direction and according to individual judgment, for the magnetic needle is not yet in use here. The quartz broken into small pieces is put into leather bags which are then carried to the surface on poles by workers whose special job this is, and from there others transport it to the mills.

Mr. Rodgers further accommodated us by accompanying us to his neighbor, Señor Don José Padilla, also a gold mine owner who received us with great cordiality and, after treating us to an excellent lunch, presented us with many valuable quartz samples and then led us to his nearby mine.

Our path led us by a small village the houses of which were hidden among amazingly high mounds of earth. The whole area reminded one of the marshy meadows of Hungary during October and April when the moles are active, except of course that the hills here are much much taller. The inhabitants were all in or around their wells where, with the help of squeaking wooden pulleys, they were pulling up sacks of gold dust, mud, or earth, while in the nearby ditches naked men, women, and children were, with untiring patience, sifting the dust or washing the mud and earth in their goat horns. It is impossible to express the pity I felt for these poor, miserable creatures and how glad I was that I am not one of these gold mine owners. The shepherd of Tarnoca with his annual earnings of ten florins is a king compared to these creatures.

In a little while we reached the mountainside where our helpful guide showed us a lead mine in a limestone formation which was crammed with petrified fossils and from which we collected some very interesting specimens. Around the top of the mountain we inspected a rich copper mine where we collected a variety of beautiful samples of copper. With the help of hard stones, Mr. Padilla crushed a few of these pieces in his hands and, after a quick wash, showed us countless numbers of gold and silver particles in them, demonstrating convincingly how rich the ore was. The main vein of the mine is imbedded in a dense limestone layer and its crumbly and battered appearance suggests that it may have been a watercourse at one time. The protruding boulders are all smooth and round, and in the mountainside there are many circular indentations which our guide called *bolsillo*, or pockets. According to him, these pockets contain the richest ones. At the entrance to the mine there are many fragments of calcium carbonate strewn about, which are usually gouged with the copper.

Continuing further, we descended on the western side of the mountain and within half an hour we were in Mr. Padilla's gold mine. Here, the ore is found in very spongy and porous stone formations which crumble even when hit lightly. From the roof and sides of the mine we tore off many pieces with our bare hands. The vein runs about horizontally from north to south in a dense layer of limestone. According to Mr. Padilla, the richest vein is always close to ground level, for after many experiments he found mining in great depth unprofitable. Here too, we saw many examples of calcium carbonate but only in rhomboid crystals. Mr. Padilla's gold mine is one of the largest and most industriously worked on the entire peninsula. The greatest problem is the lack of water in the immediate vicinity; however, an ample amount of water is collected in conduits during the winter months, when often as many as 2,000 men work in and around the mine.

It is regrettable that the annual yield and income from these mines cannot be ascertained. They are owned by the federal (Mexican) government which leases them, depending on the size of their yield, while others are the property of individuals and companies who are taxed by the government according to their earnings. It is therefore natural for both parties to withold information about their income and thus manipulate the taxes or rents to serve their best interests.

At the present time in the huge territory of the Mexican Republic, there are mints only in Mexico City and in the city of Ures and consequently miners and panners of gold are forced to sell their goods to merchants who, considering the high cost of transportation to the mints, buy them at a considerable discount. If, however the government should establish a mint in La Paz, as it has planned to do for a long time, it would be a great boost to the entire industry. Everyone would be able to convert the fruit of his labor into cash and at the right price and not be forced as now to give away his goods at miserably low prices and on credit.

During our excursion we saw numerous herds of sheep and cattle in the mountains. To give the reader an idea of the extent of cattle raising in this area, we might mention that Mr. Padilla alone owns about 40,000 sheep. Wool is not considered a valuable commodity, partly because enough cotton is grown on the land and partly on account of the coarse quality for which there is no demand. An unsheared sheepskin ordinarily sells for one-half a real and Mr. Padilla would gladly have his whole herd sheared were he offered four reals for the wool of 100 sheep.

The most important mines of the California peninsula are, however, neither the gold and silver, nor the copper and lead mines, but the famous mercury mine of Marques in the immediate vicinity of La

Paz. This mine is right in the center of the major gold and silver mines, and it seems as if Providence in its benevolence had wanted to overwhelm this region with its blessings.

The Indians have known about the mercury deposit of the peninsula since time immemorial, and for centuries they have collected cinnabar in large quantities in order to adorn themselves, and also to carry on an amazingly extensive trade with the dye, traveling as far north as to the Indians of Oregon. In spite of this, the mine came into civilized hands only a few short years ago when a Mexican captain, after personally exploring it, bought it from the Indian owners. He then formed a company to develop the mine, but owing to lack of capital it soon went bankrupt and suspended operations. A few years later an Englishman became the head of the undertaking, paid up the original company's debts, acquired the right of ownership, formed a new company, and started operations, but this time in grand style. The mine now is equipped with smelting ovens and steam engines, and employs about 1,500 workers. Close to $500,000 was invested in the venture, which so far has brought only a 2 percent return, but the company expects not only that the income will increase in a few years but that they will also recover the entire original investment.

When we arrived at the mine we found ourselves among attractive houses surrounded by lush tropical vegetation. We crossed the patio and approached the tunnel dug into the mountainside, which was the actual entrance to the mine. The tunnel has already been dug into the bowels of the mountain to a length of 2,100 feet and is ten feet by ten in height and width, lined with heavy wooden beams over its entire length. A double-railed railway in the tunnel carries carts loaded with ore from end to end, taking it directly to the smelters.

The carts were empty on their way in; so we climbed into them and were soon on our way to the land of darkness. Nothing was visible here except the light of the torch at the end of the tunnel and the dank, musty atmosphere soon enveloped us. So quickly did we get used to the change that we no longer felt it when descending to the ghastly lower pits where the breakneck hazards of our journey really began. By torchlight we proceeded along an extensively long and very damp corridor which, after a turn, led into an entry hall, a kind of cavern where in a niche we saw an altar of *Nuestra Señora*. The altar, the ornaments, the candleholders, and the cross were all made of silver and the candles are lit day and night. Here, every miner before starting a day's work, kneels and offers his soul and body unto the protection of *Nuestra Señora*.

From the entry hall we descended on a vertical ladder, if it can be called a ladder, being a long palm trunk from which the branches had been removed and onto which steps had been hacked with an axe. Descending in this manner about twenty-five feet, we stood on a slippery slab of rock from where we proceeded onto a narrow passage, in places at the very edge of gaping chasms, and descended ever deeper on a notched tree trunk. Here we stumbled along in pitch dark among stripped rocks and stones and then descended deeper again on rungs carved into stone slabs. Thus, further and further we went through numerous passageways, caverns, vaults, steps and ladders, always in total darkness and always seeing only dimly the flickering torch and candlelight in the distance, which nevertheless shone like a guiding light in the underworld, or, as in Shakespeare, like "a good deed in a naughty world."

Later, the manager of the mine was kind enough to show us a map on which the subterranean tunneling was visible in detail. The mine resembled a subterranean city with its multitude of winding and cross-sectional shafts, alleys, and corridors. To venture into this labyrinth without a guide would be like proceeding without Ariadne's thread.

The miners had named the alleys and passages after the saints but they soon had come to the end of the calendar and the newer ones were named after animals, for example, "Elephant," "Giraffe," "Bear," and so on. The fact that eighty-four pounds of candle are burned every twenty-four hours by the miners will give the reader an idea of the extent of this subterranean city.

A turn in the tunnel brought us up to the miners. One of them, standing on a wooden platform high above us, was drilling a hole to be filled with gunpowder and detonated. Blasting the rock with gunpowder seems very dangerous to me, but I was assured that no miner had ever fallen victim to it and that no mishap had ever occurred, except for minor bruises and burns, which were more the result of carelessness. It is difficult for me to see how a person can keep his balance on a thin wooden board while constantly on the move and working very hard.

The miners who drill holes in the rock in this manner accompany their work with a peculiar sound which is halfway between a moan and a sigh, and which I was told to make their job easier for them. Even so, every time we passed a work force of six to eight men, all moaning or sighing, I was so touched by pity that tears welled up in my eyes. If only there had been a song, even a funeral dirge, I could have stood it easier. But in this ghostly place these ghostly figures with their moans and sighs and the eery light given off by tallow candles stuck into the rock (which was just sufficient to make the darkness visible), I was reminded of Tantalus, so much so that I began to believe that these tortured sounds were the voices of the damned for whom there was no escape.

The miners work in groups and each group is divided into two shifts, the day shift and the night shift. Inquiring for their average life expectancy, I was told that few reach the age of forty-five and almost without exception they die of lung disease, which proves that light and fresh air is indispensable not only for plant but also for animal life.

We proceeded with shudders and met another group of workers approaching. We stepped out of their way as they were rising step by step from the seemingly bottomless depths until finally they passed before us groaning, breathing heavily, and at times reeling from the desperate exertion of muscles carrying the heavy load which bends their bodies almost in half. These are the *tenateros* or porters who carry the ore in sacks to the tunnel and place them in the carts. Like the miners, they are not burdened with superfluous clothing, for they wear only a coarse shirt, pants, and deerskin buskins.

The ore is put into a flat leather bag (*talego*) which is then fastened to the forehead of the porter by a two-inch wide strap so that the entire weight rests on the spine and shoulder. Thus the *tenatero* lugs 200 pounds of ore from rung to rung on the vertical ladder and almost everywhere in total darkness, for the lead lamp with its sickly light illuminates only the numerous precipices and gaping chasms, to remind him that one false step or slip would put him beyond human help. It is fortunate for the *tenatero* that he is alternately ascending and descending and, although the effort is the same, he carries no load when descending for otherwise, considering that he makes this trip sixteen to eighteen times a day, it is hard to imagine how he could survive the very first day.

Let us follow the *tenateros* who finally reach the tunnel and transfer their loads onto the carts. As we run after them, they emerge into the open air, where they burst into laughter from sheer relief, which is not at all surprising for the change of air also has a powerful effect on us. At the end of the rails they unload the carts as easily and effortlessly as if they were handling turnips or cabbages instead of ore. They lift and throw off the larger pieces of ore and then grab wide-bladed shovels, jump into the carts, and shovel out the small pieces of ore and soil remaining on the bottom with amazing skill and speed. Then they return with great speed on the whirling carts and continue their hazardous activities.

Another group of workers break up the ore into smaller pieces; then it is dumped onto the patio into paving-stone size and piled into heaps shaped like pyramids, while the soil is screened through a coarse wire sieve. Other workers make adobe clay out of the screened soil.

The miners are not paid a daily wage but according to the quantity of ore produced, and for this reason they work in groups of four to twelve individuals, in two shifts, one shift at night and the other during the day, so that they have a complete check on one another. The price of the ore is decided a week in advance by the management and the miners. Under such conditions they earn very little when they work on very hard rock but, on the other hand, when they hit rich and easily worked strata, their earnings greatly increase. Often an individual miner may earn as much as thirty to forty dollars a week, but many times they earn less than ten dollars, seldom less than that. The average weekly earning is about fifteen dollars a week.

Apparently the company is generous and humane in the treatment of its workers, one proof of which is that when the miners work on barren rock in order to achieve better ventilation and to reach better strata, they are paid at an agreed rate and according to the number of *vara* (about two and one-half cubic feet of rock).

The miners have nothing to do with carting the ore. It is all done by the *tenateros*, who are hired and paid for this purpose by the company. Each group of miners deposit their ore in a specific place, and it is weighed twice a week before being transported from the mine. Each group also elects a foreman who looks after the affairs of the group, collects their pay, and distributes it among the members, buys their food and clothing, supervises the work, and sees to it that everyone does his proper share.

The *tenateros'* daily wage is two dollars, the weight checkers and screeners earn one and a half dollars, the adobe mixers and blacksmiths two and a half dollars, and the carpenters three dollars. These wages do honor to the company, for they are not only just but generous, but this has little influence on the workers for they all drink and gamble. No matter how much they earn during the week, by Monday they are back where they started, without a penny in their pocket. There is no provision whatever for sickness or old age, in which case these pitiable creatures have no choice but to lie down and die like worn-out beasts of burden. Furthermore, the large majority of the work force are Indians, half-breeds, and Mexicans who are apparently the most impractical people in the world and faithfully cling to the customs of their forefathers, firmly convinced that "if I take care of today, Providence will take care of the morrow."

At this point I should like to acquaint the reader with the method of smelting the ore, and for this purpose I have drawn one of the eighteen smelters. They are new in design, were installed about a year ago, and have been in constant operation ever since with good results.

The smelting of mercury from cinnabar is the simplest operation imaginable. The ore compartment (B) is filled with cinnabar and is tightly covered. A blazing fire is ignited in the furnace (A) and through openings in the brickwall the heat penetrates into the ore compartment and completely envelops the cinnabar. In a short time mercury in gaseous form is released, which through holes in the wall opposite enters the compression chambers (C), rising to the top of one and descending to the bottom of the next one, which the arrows in the sketch clearly indicate. After passing through thirteen compression chambers, the gas cools and solidifies into mercury metal. In order to prevent any of the gas escaping from the last compression chamber, it is passed through a large receptacle filled with cold water (D), and if, in spite of all this, any gas still escapes, there is a vertical pipe in the chimney through which there is a constant drip of water through a screen onto the gas, completely cooling and compressing it as it ascends the chimney.

As soon as the mercury cools, it immediately drops to the bottom and, through pipes installed for this purpose in the compression chambers, it flows into a trough (E) from which it is conducted into a caldron (F) at the end of the building and packed into hermetically sealed flasks of seventy-five pounds. Each of these flasks costs forty-five dollars locally, or one florin and thirty pennies per pound.

As I mentioned before, La Paz's location is picturesque, especially when viewed from the sea. The houses are attractive, with flat asphalt roofs, painted in gaudy colors. Since local commerce is consid-

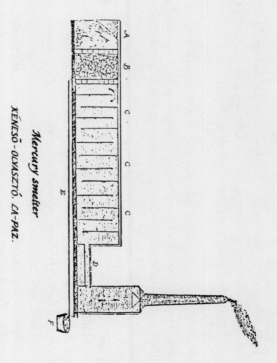

Mercury smelter
XÉNESÖ - OLVASZTÓ. LA-PAZ.

17. Mercury Smelter

erable, there is a lively traffic on its streets all day long. One meets everywhere busy people bustling about. Most of the streets are laid out in symmetrical squares. The plaza or main square is especially worth mentioning. The area of this large square is about ten acres, one side of which is occupied by an attractive cathedral, the residence of the bishop, and a seminary, while the opposite side is lined with decorative buildings, the City Hall, and the offices of the provincial government. On the other two sides are the library, grammar school, customs house, and many private homes. The square is planted with trees, and there is a beautiful fountain in the center fed by one of the cold springs from the nearby mountains. The Plaza, the best-known place in La Paz, is where the cream of the local society gathers every night. Twice a week the band of the Mexican regiment stationed in the city gives a concert. At such times, if judged by appearances alone, the population does not seem to be poor, but rather quite affluent. This situation is further underscored by the fact that La Paz is independent of external commerce owing to the wide variety and volume of its products. For example, the breakfast table of the wealthy is made of smoothly polished cedarwood, covered with a cloth of fine quality snow white cotton, set with heavy silverware, and platters stacked with a variety of meats—lamb, beef, venison—plus fish, eggs, milk, butter, white bread, coffee, sugar, figs, oranges and many other things, all produced within the immediate vicinity of the city. Guests at such breakfasts are seated by the host in different kinds of mahogany chairs, made locally of wood grown on his own plantation. The Indian servants pick grapes and make a good quality wine. They also supply the household abundantly with tobacco and all kinds of tropical fruit. The climate is so favorable that horses and all domestic animals graze in the open all year around and therefore their keep costs nothing. The material for the scant and thin clothes worn the year around is also grown, spun, woven, dyed, and sewn locally. Silver is not valued too highly by the Creole and is used only for spurs, saddle ornaments, and tableware. Gold coins are fashioned into earrings, crosses, hearts, and images of the Virgin for the Indian girls. In consequence, the population of La Paz is just as lazy and lethargic as any other Spanish American people, for under such an hospitable climate few people have the incentive to acquire more than is absolutely necessary.

My previous observation about the day long hustle and bustle in the city applies of course only to the poor working people and the merchants. Most of the latter are foreigners who exert every effort to achieve their aim, which is to get rich.

All these activities have scarcely any influence on the Creoles, the descendants of the Castilian conquerors, who own most of the land and their serflike servants. They live just like the feudal gentry in Hungary. All they do is eat, drink, and idle about. They look down with supreme disdain on anyone rushing about or working to earn money.

To illustrate the smug self-indulgence of a *hidalgo* of La Paz, it is best to describe his daily routine.

Early in the morning he climbs out of bed and flings himself into a hammock while his wife settles on a couch next to him. The children all sit around on the carpet, Turkish fashion, in their night clothes. An Indian servant girl enters and serves every member of the family a cup of cocoa or chocolate on a silver platter. After this she brings in glowing embers, also on a silverplatter, on which the lady lights a cigar first for her husband and then for herself. While they smoke their cigars, there is a lively conversation among the members of the family, after which the husband leisurely (he has no reason to hurry) dons his cotton pants and cotton jacket, puts on his shoes, straw hat, and strolls to visit one of his neighbors, where he will drink more chocolate and smoke more cigars.

At twelve o'clock noon, a low table is set in the center of the dining room and the family sits down to breakfast. The wife next to her husband, the children next to the mother, and the hunting dogs all around on the carpet. *Chupe* (sweet potato) and grilled chops are the first course. The master serves himself first and throws the bones across the table to the dogs while the children start pitching the bones into contact with the flying missiles. Following the paternal example, the children start pitching the bones and this time the *padre* and *madre* duck under the table to avoid them. The dogs fight and bite each other while the second course is brought in, which consists of diced, boneless meat. This is followed by a richly spiced meatbroth, then a variety of desserts and fruits, and finally coffee and chocolate.

After breakfast the master sheds his jacket, trousers, and shoes and stretches out on the hammock. The wife first lights a cigar for him, then lights her own, and settles down on the couch. The dogs also deposit themselves on couches for they don't take kindly to the fleas on the floor, the maid lowers the curtains, closes the doors, and takes the children for a walk.

At three in the afternoon the church bells begin to ring, calling the faithful to prayer. The master jumps up, stretches himself, yawning, the dogs follow his example, while the wife shouts for fire to light the cigars for her husband and herself.

For dinner, which is usually around four o'clock, the same dishes are served as for breakfast, amidst the same ceremonies, including the loafing in the hammock and the cigar smoking. Around five o'clock an Indian servant brings a saddled horse to the front of the veranda and the master, after arming his boots with formidable silver spurs, leaps into the saddle and rides over to one his neighbors. When he gets there, he takes his hat off before the open window and greets the ladies: *"Buenos tardes, señoritas."* They immediately appear on the veranda and while one of them lights a cigar for the caballero, another prepares a glass of lemonade. After a short chat, the caballero tips his hat and rides over to another acquaintance where the same scene is repeated, and so it goes on all afternoon. At sundown he returns home, hands the reins over to his Indian servant, throws off his clothes, and stretches out on the hammock. The chocolate and cigar routine is repeated, and the rest of the evening and a good part of the night is spent either in strolling or dancing.

Seeing all this, and personally experiencing the exceptional hospitality of the Creoles to strangers, it would seem that their life is the most attractive and happy in the world. It may be so for the natives, but the North American and European who has learned to live a productive and intellectually satisfying life, would soon be bored by this life style and quickly realize that tropical life is not for him. Isolated from kindred spirits and removed from any useful activity, this kind of existence is nothing but retirement, which may be attractive to some, but is actually closer to nonexistence with which no intellectually active person can be satisfied for a long period of time. It is not life, but merely vegetation.

Scientific institutions are nonexistent on the peninsula and what education there is can hardly be called by that name, although there are a few elementary schools in La Paz. They are, however, of such poor quality that they promise little future for popular education. On the peninsula just as in Hungary in former times, instruction is thrust haphazardly at the pupils, without regard for age and capacity.

Literature, too, is neglected, as indicated by the fact, that only fifty books have been printed so far in La Paz, and three-fourths of these are mostly translations of religious themes and textbooks. Journalism is represented by two weekly publications, one of which is the official government publication (*Bolletin Official*) and the other is the journal of the opposition, *El Clamor Publico* or *Public Opinion*, which hardly publishes anything but election news and advertisements, while the former contains only official decrees and congressional announcements. Neither publishes foreign news, and when they make an exception and do so, the facts are so distorted that one is amazed by the ignorance of the editors.

Out of curiosity, I leafed through the 1849 volume of *El Clamor Publico* and found many ridiculous statements published about my homeland.

Although I have discussed in some detail the geography and plant life of the peninsula, I have deliberately omitted any mention of the fauna, especially the birds. I wanted to deal with them separately. About nine-tenths of the Tejon bird species exist on the peninsula also, but in addition there are about 100 different birds, according to my calculations, a large number of which make their permanent home here. The others migrate seasonally from South and Central America, but never fly as far as Tejon. The reason is natural and obvious. Among naturalists it is a well-known fact that migratory birds, on their way either south or north, follow the great bodies of water, and when they

149

have flown a long enough distance and find a suitable climate, they alight in valleys offering favorable conditions either for nesting or for spending the winter. Thus, many northern birds unable to stand the frigid climate of northern Canada, move southward in late autumn, follow the Colorado River and the Purple Sea, and settle down on these shores for the winter. In the spring they cannot endure the heat of the peninsula or of Sonora, and return to the north by the same route. Central and South American birds accustomed to moderate climates leave their habitat at the onset of the summer, follow the coastline to the north, and alight in the coastal valleys of the Purple Sea. They nest there and in the autumn return with their offspring.

It is evident from all this that there is an unparalleled opportunity here for ornithologists, even if we fail to take into consideration that at least 300 different species of birds inhabit the peninsula and without a doubt new ones may be discovered by the application of diligent and precise methods. There is hardly a more favorable location in America than the vicinity of La Paz and Todos Santos to apply oneself to that most important task—the fundamental determination of the geographical classification of the birds of the American continent.

The bird life of the peninsula truly surpasses anything that may be seen in the northern parts of America. The number of singing birds of the most brilliant hues is enormous. The traveler is lost in astonishment. In Europe the belief is universal that American birds may have brilliant coloration, but they do not sing. I do not know what this notion is based on because nowhere in the entire world are there as many singing birds as in any one part of America. It is hard to imagine more charming singing birds than the America finch, or thrush, or blackbird. They have hundreds of different varieties many of which, while not as famous as singers as the European nightingale, have nevertheless an incomparably more varied repertoire, and therefore greater singing ability. Some of these, for example, are the *Orpheus polyglottus* and *Orpheus montanus*; the *Toxostoma redivivum* and *Toxostoma curvirostris*; the *Cardinalis sinuatus*; the *Pyranga rubra*; the *Carpoddcus frontalis* and many, many others.*

Besides these, the traveler is struck by the many colibris (hummingbirds) and their gorgeous coloring. Wherever flowers bloom or their aroma is noticeable, these tiny birds are present in large num-

*Thrashers, finches, tanagers, cardinals.

bers. In promenades and gardens, meadows and woods, over waters, they flutter everywhere in every size and color, from the size of a swallow to the tiniest, which are considerably smaller than the common domestic bee. At times, one can glimpse their twists and turns as they chase each other but they fly with such lightning speed that the eye can hardly follow their movements. At other times, they make many turns as they rise higher and higher until suddenly, like a bullet, they dive down into the flowers, humming and buzzing. Then again they may perch in large flocks on the dry branches of bushes, preening their feathers with their long beaks as they proudly enjoy their own blindingly splendid colors. Then with total nonchalance they fly to the flower blossoms where they engage in an ardent battle with the insects, especially the bees. This writer observed them time and time again as their tufts and back feathers bristle and color with fury as they do battle with large wasps, which usually ends in victory; they chase the wasps from the flowers, using their long, sharp bills.

Europeans, who can only see stuffed specimens in museums, always admire the gorgeous plumage of these birds, but of course it cannot be compared to the live birds seen in perpetual motion in their native habitat. This writer is considered a skilled bird-collector who in the last few years has stuffed several hundred colibris, yet he must admit that the finest example of his skill are mere shadows of the live models. This is so because the barbs and downs of the feathers change color depending upon whether the birds are viewed from the front, rear, or sides, and since every barb revolves around the shaft of the feather, the color becomes iridescent with the slightest movement of the wing. For example, the local red colibri (*Trochilus rufus*) changes from flame red to green gold, then again to indigo blue and an orange yellow as its wings vibrate.

There are very few people in my fatherland who have ever seen a live colibri, and although many Hungarians have traveled in America, I am certain that nine-tenths of them paid no heed to them, even though countless numbers may have fluttered around them. To properly observe the colibri one should first know their habits, habitat, and especially one's ears must be attuned to hearing and distinguishing the sound of their flight. One could live among them for years without recognizing them, thinking that the humming and buzzing creatures are wasps, bees, or other insects. But once we know their habits and mode of life, their sounds, we can detect the tree or flowers they inhabit, their numbers, and the species they belong to, even from a distance of a quarter of a mile.

Since nothing has been published about them in Hungary, and knowing that there are many who would like to know more about the colibri, I will be happy to provide the reader with all the data available.

The colibri are exclusively American birds. Until recently there were about 100 different species known to natural science, a number considered extremely large, but in the last few years unknown areas have been explored and new species of colibri have been discovered in such unexpected numbers that the scientific world was astounded. Until recently, no department of ornithology was able to show a genus so profuse, even though natural scientists have been unremittingly active for nearly a century. At the present time there are no less than 307 different and completely identified species of colibri.

Many believe that the colibri is native to the Americas below the equator, especially to Brazil. This, however, is erroneous because Brazil and other South American countries produce the poorest representatives compared to the beauty and number of colibri in Mexico and Central America. The genus extends throughout the Americas from the Falkland Islands to the northernmost parts of Canada, and specimens have been found even at the edges of the Arctic Ocean. It is the region between New Granada and the Purple Sea, or the lands between the 9° and 30° north latitude, including the West Indies, however, which produce the most numerous and colorful representatives.

Every shade and nuance known to the fine arts is represented in the colibri. In addition, many of the species glow with all the radiance of precious stones. There are others, however, which are unpretentiously plain, of solid color, without iridescence. To these species belong the large black ones, a few red ones, some of the color of snuff, and some emerald green.

As to size, there are many variations. A Brazilian species for example, (*Trochilus giganteus*) which is all black with blue wings, is about the size of a Hungarian snipe, and many species are not much smaller than these. Others are the size of a swallow, but the great majority are so tiny that many of them are smaller than the common bee, and there are hundreds and hundreds of insects which are larger than most colibri.

They also vary greatly in structure. Some species are of delicate frame, while others are comparatively solid and stocky. Many have exceptionally long bills, which are often much longer than the bird itself.

The *Trochilus ensiferus*, for example, have such extraordinary long bills that museum visitors need to be persuaded that they are natural growths and not artifices. These long bills have a function: to extract food from the inside of the bell-shaped flowers that grow everywhere in great abundance in the tropics. There are many species with comparatively shorter bills, but there are hardly two species that have bills of identical size and structure. Some are straight and long, others short, while with still others curl down like a sickle. Some species have bills that turn upward like a sickle, which gives them a most comical appearance.

In addition to the bill, colibris have other special appendages. One species, for example, has tails that are three to four times as long as the body, while others have comparatively short tails, but the two side feathers are exceptionally long and quite thin, with paddle- or spoon-shaped ends. Furthermore, the feet of this species are thickly covered with feathers all the way to the claws. From the standpoint of nature's economy, it is difficult to guess the purpose of this peculiarity.

Compared to other birds, the colibris' wings are long and powerful and, knowing their life style, it is evident that they are built for continuous and quite rapid flight.

By now it is established beyond a doubt that the colibri are insectivorous, and for my part, I agree with Mr. Gould's* definitive statement that the honey and dew in the flower chalice serve merely as their drink, that the birds extract no sustenance from them. The bird's tongue is its tool, used to suck the dew and to collect the insects; it is constructed to fulfill this function. It is long and contains two tubes (resembling the double barrel of a rifle) that function as a muscular suction pipe, the tip of which is forked; the tongue of some species is notched on the sides, doubtless to facilitate the collection of small and soft insects. Also, the colibri is able to thrust its tongue quite far out, like the woodpecker, and this enables it to explore the very bottom of the deepest flower chalice.

The throat and neck are usually the most brilliant, although in some species the crest, and in others the underside and wings, are of a dazzling splendor. The upper part is usually much plainer.

*John Gould (1804–1881), famous British ornithologist.

In many places where the colibri live in large numbers, certain species are scattered over a large territory while others crowd into much narrower and well-defined borders. Certain species thrive under the hottest tropical skies, while others prosper only in the valleys, and still others in the highest mountains and plateaus, and there are species known to be found only in the snowcapped Andes.

Scant attention was paid to the colibri of California and Mexico until quite recently, and no claim can be made that they are sufficiently known as yet, even though numerous species exist in these countries, and periodically even more visit the environs of the Sierra Nevada. When I arrived at Tejon last year, I saw only a few, but at the beginning of August they arrived unexpectedly and in such great numbers that every flowering tree and bush was literally covered with them. I offered rewards to the Indians, and acquired many live specimens. Very quickly I had no less than seventy in my possession which I kept in cages. I managed to keep most of them alive for months. Had I had the time to give them more attention and proper care, I haven't the slightest doubt that I could have shipped them alive to Europe; but I had to be away for several days and they all perished, due to the carelessness of the individual in whose care I left them. I learned from this experiment that, although the entire genus is of very excitable nature, and when free would not permit the proximity of another species without resistance, the various species lived in perfect harmony in cages, even when as sometimes happened, a tiny one would land on the beak of a larger one. Nonchalantly, it preened its feathers while the larger bird paid no attention to the affront.

The coloring of the sexes is amazingly different in some species, so much so that even first-rate naturalists have difficulty determining the sex of an individual bird. For example, in the case of the *Cynanthus Lucifer*, a species found in prolific numbers on the peninsula, it would have been impossible to recognize the male and female as belonging to the same species, if their discoverer had not found them together and proved it after dissection. The male is golden green with a bronze red throat and protruding, long, yellow feathers on the sides; the female, however, is ash-colored and half the size of the male.

As a rule they nest and hatch in July. The nests are proofs of the remarkable ingenuity of these little birds. Some are built of small particles of moss or roots resembling threads of silk, others are constructed from cotton or from petals and shreds of flowers, and many species weave their nests exclusively with spider web. The placement of the nests is also unusual. Many hang theirs among thorns and on cactus leaves, others weave them on the outermost leaves of bushes and tree branches. Some build them on thoroughly dry trees and bushes, others on vertical rock walls, in spots where no swallow could hang its nest. In fact, I often saw their nests on the smoothly whitewashed walls of houses. Without exception, they lay two eggs in the nest. The colibri egg is snowhite and, considering the size of the bird, quite large. Male and female build the nest together and alternate sitting on the eggs which hatch in twenty days. In ten days the young birds leave the nest and sit for several days on nearby branches, until finally they take off with their parents. The bird will never leave its nest when there is an egg in it unless it is relieved by its partner. The pair perform this task so faithfully that on such occasions anyone can approach and catch them in the nest. It often happened that I would reach in the nest with my hand with its beak, but would not move, and when I caught it, stroked it, and put it back in its nest, it still did not fly away but remained sitting, burrowing as deeply as it could.

If one partner is sitting on the egg, the other always stays in the vicinity and never fails to protect the partner against attackers from the bird world, and at times even against snakes. On such occasions these birds are extremely interesting, for under the influence of fear and fury their movements are so swift that the eye is incapable of following, and only the ear can hear the drone and buzz. The pair would attack and most of the time chase away ravens, jades, hawks, and kites without discrimination, for the sharp, needlelike, long bill is no mean weapon, especially when flying with bulletlike speed at the enemy, aiming for its eyes.

Nothing compares however to the rage of the colibri when a stranger of their own species intrudes during the nesting period. They are so jealous that they turn into perfect furies. With the throat puffed and their crest and back feathers ruffled they engage in a battle in the air amidst sounds of shrieks until one or both drops to the ground. In Tejon I have witnessed such combats many times; in one particular instance, under my window in a heavy rain, I thought that even one drop would suffice to knock the fighters to the ground. But not so, they fought on for at least ten minutes, when one of them dropped from exhaustion and the other triumphantly sat next to the nest, viewing with great satisfaction the defeated foe.

Such combats are mentioned in the works of almost every naturalist, especially those who have personally observed the little battlers in their own habitat. In particular, the small but rather interesting volume of Philip Gosse on the colibri of Jamaica contains the following description of the colibri battle:*

A mango colibri (*Trochilus mango*), one of the common and most beautiful West Indian species took possession for days of a malay tree (*Eugenia malaccensis*) under my window, ceaselessly plundering its beautiful flowers. One morning, however, quite unexpectedly, another bird of the same species appeared, resulting in some extraordinarily interesting warlike maneuvers between the tiny creatures. At first they started to chase each other with tremendous speed amidst the branches and foliage, until at an appropriate moment one cornered the other in an opening, then with swishing wings colliding, they attacked each other. Entangled, they whirled around in the air at times almost touching the ground with such great speed that their twists and turns seemed like a rainbow in the air, making them indistinguishable. It took me a little time to see clearly what happened, when just a few inches from me a new battle started. One of them caught with his bill the bill of the other and thus joined together they were flying up and down with unimaginable speed, continually whirling and twisting. For several minutes they carried on this amazing combat until at last, rolling on the ground totally exhausted, they separated, sat on some branches and rested for some minutes. Then they started to chirp again which was probably a new challenge for instantly they clashed again. During a rest period an unfortunate brown creeper (*Certhia flaveola*) sounded its sad song and pecking, whereupon the two battlers immediately joined forces to attack the common enemy, which flew off terrified, finding refuge in a nearby tree. Hardly was the creeper chased away than the allies turned again on each other, starting a new fight and this continued without a stop until one of them was defeated and forced to break off. The war, for that is what it was, with its series of battles, lasted for more than an hour and both birds were male.

*Philip H. Gosse (1810–1888), English naturalist, *Manual of Marine Zoology*, 2 vols. (London, 1855–56).

Coming to the end of our allotted time in La Paz, we packed and at noon on May 16 started our return trip on the eastern side of the peninsula.

We left La Paz with great regret, for we left many good friends behind who had done everything to make our sojourn a pleasant one and helped us to achieve the objective of our trip. Mr. Rochambeau, together with his family, were particularly gracious to us, we owe them much gratitude, and we shall not soon forget his hospitality. We are also beholden to Dr. Leatherman, the surgeon of the first dragoon regiment of the U.S., especially for the very valuable data about the Tejon Indians.

As we traveled a few miles in a northerly direction, we ascended from the fertile valley to a higher plateau where shifting sands were everywhere along the Purple Sea, which was always visible. Along our route we saw many ruins; in many places the area was covered for miles with fragments of tile; the foundations of the houses were thickly covered with sand or buried in the sand dunes. But the traces of *acequias* or irrigation ditches which were used by residents of former times to irrigate the region were clearly distinguishable, and our eyes could follow them for miles and miles.

The sand was damp in many places, especially in the lowlands where salty matter bubbled up under the footsteps of our mules. At such times looking back it seemed as if the entire area was covered with dew. Due to this circumstance, the footprints of herds could be seen and traced for days and experienced natives could tell with certainty when and how many animals had passed through here.

Toward evening we passed near a large pile of stones which seemed to be man-made, and when we rode up to it it turned out to be a sixty-square-foot edifice built of adobe and native stone with two rows of gun holes, but there was no trace of doors or windows. After an extensive and tiring search we could not even find remnants of furniture, household or farm utensils, with the exception of a huge seashell covered with carvings and scripts. There was no sign at all of any hewn wood, and the ends of the cross beams in the walls—the rest of them had burned out long ago—were natural, round tree trunks. The interior showed all the signs of a fire and because of it the walls had lost much of their original aspect.

At sundown we passed through the small village of Marques,

which consisted of many one-, two- and three-story houses, some of which had doors and windows, especially the ones which were built since the nearby mercury mines had been working. They were meant to accommodate the miners who crowded into Marques on Sundays and holidays.

A few miles from Marques we settled down for the night in a camp whose inhabitants, most of them Indians, provided us with an ample supply of bananas, melons, and green corn for our mules. I questioned some of the more intelligent about the origin of the ruins, in the hope of learning some of their ancient history, but in vain, for none of them were able to furnish me with more information than my own investigation. One of them told us a story about it, but it was so improbable that I do not consider it worth repeating.

Around ten o'clock the next day we reached the village of San Lazaro, consisting of a four-story building. Here we rested for a few hours and fed and watered our cattle. The road between Marques and San Lazaro was the same uninteresting, barren wasteland as the one yesterday. Excepting for the thousands of cattle and horses licking the salt flats in the distance, there was no sign of any plant or animal life.

San Lazaro has a population of about 400. Like the people of La Joya, they get to their homes only by climbing ladders. The padre is a full blooded Indian, a disciple of the Jesuits, and in many respects a highly intelligent person. In one corner of the communal building, as is customary in such villages, there is a nice little church, the altar of which is richly decorated with silver ornaments, and on its walls are masterly Spanish paintings portraying the saints in their various occupations. There is no sign of a school and the reader will undoubtedly be surprised to learn that among the 400 people there are only two who can read and write, the padre and the *alcalde*.

The rooms and verandas are filled with bananas, melons, plantains, squash, beans, and peaches and the walls are literally jammed with paprika strung on cords which according to our calculations, amounted to at least 1,000 bushels. This is a clear indication of how much they like paprika, since there are more than two bushels for each man, woman, and child.

We also observed here the making of *pinole*, which is much favored although somewhat of a luxury food of the peninsula. It is made in the following manner: the milky kernels of maize are collected, dried, ground, and then mixed with sugar (where sugar cane is grown, sugar is made from the green cornstalk stripped of its leaves) and water, and shaped into small cakes. One-fourth of any of these cakes, when diluted with water in a gourd, makes not only a refreshing but also a nourishing drink. It can also make bad water drinkable and pleasant tasting.

Of domestic animals we saw only a few: dogs and chickens around the house or village, even though the villagers have many cattle, mules, horses, and sheep; but they graze throughout the year under the supervision of shepherds and are seldom driven to the village.

When we finally climbed down from the building, we saw a woman under the shade of a poplar tree. She was sitting cross-legged with the soles of her feet turned upward. Between the big toe and the next one there was an eighteen inch long spindle with a four inch long bobbin on its top, which she was periodically rotating with her fingers with amazing speed and skill. Following this operation the spindle always gained a few yards of coarse yarn. We saw then how yarn is spun around here. Now we were curious to learn how they weave the yarn. We observed a young lad, lazing in the sun, getting on his feet and opening a roll—which at first seemed to me to be a casing only—then sticking four sticks in the ground. He tied the yarn to their tops and in less time than it takes to read these lines he started to weave with the aid of a tiny spindle resembling a grindstone.

In the afternoon we covered only eighteen miles and reached San Luiz Gonzaga, a four-storied village, where we settled down for the night. Our route led us through a comparatively fertile area, in many places amidst lush gardens, which proved to us that, although far removed from the civilized world, the people here are peaceful and industrious. The white man rarely, and then only accidentally, turns up in this corner of the world and is always received by the natives with kindness and brotherly love, and should he be in need, they provide him with food, clothing, and horses. Alcohol is not imbibed by the natives, with the possible exception of their leaders, and so they are spared the long list of evils caused by immoderate drinking.

The entire seacoast from La Paz all the way to 28° north latitude is inhabited by one Indian nation whose members are the direct descendants of the once famous Marijopo Indians. For more than a century they have been living in ordered communities and industriously

159

cultivating the land, often against great obstacles. Their numbers are uncertain, but having visited their villages I estimate them to be about 5,000.

The alcalde of San Luiz Gonzaga is Don Jose Messias, who like all other magistrates, is appointed by the governor in La Paz. They hold the office for a term of three years, when they are either re-appointed or removed, and someone else is appointed in their place. The people have no voice therefore in the selection of the leaders. All the same, I must admit that the alcaldes, judges, police chiefs, and justices of peace whom I got to know were all honest and intelligent men, who seemed to care for the welfare of the community, and I hardly think that the village of San Luiz Gonzaga could choose a more worthy leader than Señor Messias.

We hardly settled down when we were surrounded by the entire population bringing large amounts of fruits and food for sale. They immediately organized horse races and there was so much noise and clatter that I had to interrupt my meteorological observations and the measurement of longitude and latitude. The hoofbeats on the spongy ground influenced the mercury so much even at a distance of 400 to 500 paces, that I was unable to focus a single star in the mirror. Moreover the news had spread that I knew something about the stars and my tent was besieged by a crowd on horseback. It increased by the minute, with new spectators rushing in.

The men wore straw hats, knee-length, striped pants of a light-weight material, deerskin buskins, and capes of stripped fabric, which served as an upper garment. The only dress the women wore was a tuniclike garment of red or yellow thin material reaching well above the ankles. Both men and women were attractive both in figure and face. The long black hair in braids, the dark eyes, aquiline nose and cherry-red lips, complimented their stately, taller than average, figures.

Having finished the trading at last, the entire population settled down around the fires, endlessly chattering and having fun, until midnight, amidst so much noise that the ground seemed to be shaking under their loud laughter. Dr. Winston, a member of our party, was the special butt of their amusement, for he wore spectacles, something totally unknown and hard to grasp by these simple people. Young women were especially apprehensive at his approach for it was rumored among them that with his spectacles the doctor could see through their thin clothing and more than once they fled en masse. Finally, when the matter took a disquieting turn and was no longer a joke, after much persuasion and presents we placed the specs on the nose of an old woman, who having learned their use, became convinced that they cannot see through clothing, told the girls so and quieted them. Just the same the girls kept shaking their heads as if the explanation was not quite convincing, and when the doctor put on his glasses again, many of them ran away once again.

Having been told by the people that no water is to be found for the next thirty miles, at our request they supplied us with gourds, as everyone of us was anxious to carry as much water as possible. Naturally, the price of gourds kept rising, keeping step with the demand. For example, the first gourd I bought for a string of glass beads, for the second I had to pay four, and I could hardly get the third one for eight strings, four of which had to be the color of gold to fulfill the bargain. While such beads cost only pennies in San Francisco, considering their actual value here on the peninsula, it is clear that the gourds were much overpriced, for normally eight strings of glass beads buy a fairly good horse.

Next morning after watering our mules, we continued our wandering in a northwesterly direction. In a little while reached a pitahaya grove which was crisscrossed with salt lakes, following which we struggled through a sandy desert covered in places with fragments of granite, and as we were progressing, the elevation of the terrain was rising, but hardly noticably. There was no sign of any animal or plant life, except a few dwarf laurels, and some miserable looking acacias.

Our trip was very tiring because of the deep sand and horrible heat. There was no indication of water anywhere and by noon our animals were so thirsty and tired that when two acacia trees appeared on our trail all our mules rushed to them to tear apart and chew the green branches.

Continuing, we soon got to a creek which was so dry, however, that there was not a single moist spot in its bed. Then we again reached a high plateau after which our route led us into a low, black mountain range which was strewn with small chips of basalt and in many places signs of agate, chalcedony, fused quartz, and limestone. On the hilltop we came upon a sizable granite boulder covered with what appeared to be hieroglyphic-like symbols. From this peak we had a surprising view of the nearby Purple Sea and noted with satisfaction that we were only

161

a few miles from the nearest settlement where we would find ample water for our animals.

Descending from the hills, we crossed a plain covered with gravel of basalt and soon found ourselves in Dolores, at the mouth of a creek, a three-story village which was only a stone's throw from the sea. The village here, too, is built of adobe and is accessible only by ladders. In addition, the square structure is surrounded with a ditch, fifteen feet wide and fifteen feet deep, which is edged from end to end with three rows of sharp stakes for greater protection against hostile Indians. In every direction around the village there are extensive gardens where few tropical fruits grow. Due to the higher elevation, plantings of the moderate climate flourish; for example good quality grapes, peaches, figs, and yellow plums, as well as maize, barley, and other plants are grown in large quantities.

Before going on, we paid a visit to Señor Chavez, the alcalde, to pay for the barley consumed by our mules, and we were introduced on this occasion to the ladies assembled by the alcalde's wife. The ladies' faces were thickly coated with some sort of a white paint, so that only the natural colors of their gleaming black eyes and red lips showed through. Later we found out that the makeup is not for cosmetic purposes but to protect the skin against the burning sunrays.

The ladies were quite chatty and very hospitable; they presented us with basketfuls of cigarillos, pitchers of honey, and strings of paprika so heavy that we could hardly carry them.

One of the ladies' peculiar customs was, that each time they lit their cigars, they first asked our permission with a charming flip of the hand to their straw hats and the words *"con su licencia Señor."* Should an aged patriarch enter the room, they would all stand up, take a deep bow, raise their hats, and cease to utter a word until the aged one gave permission with a flip of the hand, or left the room.

Late in the afternoon we started out again and after a few miles arrived in the tiny village of Cananas. It consisted of a building barely fifty feet square which seemed to serve only as a fishing camp for a few Indians. All around and on the seashore we saw many nets and fish baskets spread out for drying. Leaving Cananas we found ourselves among sand dunes, ascending gradually to the crest of the barren hillocks. By sundown we descended the northern slopes into a deep gully lined with creosote and artemisia bushes, where we saw partridges by the thousands. They were so tame that when we fired a rifle into a covey, only three or four flew away and they, too, alighted again twenty to twenty-five feet away. This one (*Ortyx squamosa*) is one of the smallest of the California species, not much larger than the European quail. We found it tasted very good. The feathers are silver grey with a white crest and black wings and the meat is snow-white.

Late at night we reached the small village of Cuepo where we spent the night.

Next morning we left very early, for we wanted to arrive in Loreto in time to see everything. Loreto is the famous shrine on the peninsula, and being the high season for the pilgrimage, we intended to see as much as the time at our disposal permitted.

We did not have to use our spurs, because our mules, as if sensing our intention, started out with a fast gallop and advanced on the plain as swiftly as possible.

In a short time we reached Galiteo Creek where we watered our mules. On the creek banks there were indications of coal of coarse quality, mixed with sand and gravel. Wading across, the trail led us into a deep ravine and to the base of a fifty-foot-high cliff which, from the distance, appeared surprisingly to resemble a man-made structure, having openings like doors and windows. As we were gazing at nature's caprice, some pilgrims who were well acquainted with the place joined us, and obstinately maintained that the cliff wall was part of a castle built by Montezuma. In spite of their insistence, however, we were convinced that not even Montezuma was powerful enough to create such a gigantic structure, which would have done justice to the Cyclops.

Nearing the town we overtook a *carreta* which was loaded with beautiful black grapes, intended for the pilgrims' refreshment. We persuaded the Indians, however, that our silver was as good as that of the pilgrims and so soon we were munching on the grapes.

Around nine o'clock we reached a hot spring known as Ojo Caliente de Loreto, where some Indians were bathing and washing. To our regret our thermometers were all packed and we could not measure the temperature of the spring, but ten to fifteen steps from it our hands could not stand the heat and right at the spring the water must have reached the boiling point. The composition of the area around the springs is reddish clay mixed with sand and the basins are full of petrified matter which resemble the most exquisite coral both in structure and colors.

Collecting numerous samples of the stones and enough water, we went on, and in a matter of minutes we were on a hilltop from where we had a good view of Loreto spread out before us. We soon arrived without any incident. We were just in time, for a procession was circling the church with numerous lit candles and crosses. Dismounting, we joined the procession and, amidst the ringing of bells, followed them into the church.

Women were sitting cross-legged on the floor on the right side of the main altar wrapped in their *rebozos* (a shawl of heavy fabric worn by women of all ranks all over Latin America). The rest of the church was filled with men who were standing, except when the ceremony required them to kneel. The interior of the church is long and narrow with a high and pointed dome. At the base two cross-like branches on the right and left side of the altar serve as sacristies. On both sides of the altar two lifesize wax figures of friars stand, their heads cropped close, except for a wreath-like crown of hair. One was dressed in a blue, the other in a white cassock with a white, fringed cord around the waist. Above the altar there is a surprisingly beautiful oil painting, portraying the patron saint of the church and the place—the Virgin Mary—and numerous mirrors and pictures of the saints are hung around it as well as in other parts of the church. Also, there are countless numbers of silver hearts and other trifles donated by the pilgrims in honor of the patron saint, or in fulfillment of their vows, or sometimes as offerings to cure their sickness and to protect them from evil in the future.

There is a large, round, stained-glass window behind the altar through which the rays of the sun penetrate and mingle with thick smoke of incense, creating an atmosphere of beatitude, particularly around the altar, where countless numbers of multicolored candles are burning, and where three priests together with their assistants celebrate divine services, each one in his richly gilded and vividly woven vestments.

From one of the sacristies wild sounding music is continuously heard, but the musicians are not seen. In addition, the chanting of the devout audience, and the periodic ringing of the bells created in us a peculiar and unusual impression which stayed with us for several days, so that weeks after at night we still seemed to be hearing the bells, the music, and singing of Loreto.

At the end of the service we moved to the plaza, for in Spanish America that is the best place to learn about the characteristics of the people. Soon we found ourselves among a multitude of people, and the entire noisy scene reminded me of a village fair in Hungary. In tents, on tables, benches, even on the bare ground, were blankets, baskets and all kinds of articles for sale. Everyone tried to buy a memento of the Mary of Loreto for loved ones at home.

In addition, there were whole rows of tents filled with food stuff, for even pilgrims cannot live on praying and singing alone. When the devotions are over they are apt to get hungry and eat and drink with as good an appetite as the non-pilgrims. Evidently most of the pilgrims felt this way because the food tents were besieged, and everywhere one could see men, women, and children standing or walking by the tents, munching roast chicken, partridge, beef tongue, or any other food they could get. Bakery tents were numerous and their bread would do justice to the finest European baker. All the articles of food were extremely inexpensive.

We had not walked for long before the number and liveliness of the card tables struck us. Card playing is a passion all over California, but nowhere have I seen it displayed to the degree it is here. On the plaza, on the streets, on the steps of houses and churches, everywhere we heard "*monte*," "*monte*," "*monte*." We were surrounded by groups standing or sitting, so absorbed in the play that it was impossible not to stop and stare.

Monte is an exclusively Spanish game played with cards especially made for it. There are forty-four cards (four kings, four queens, four knights, four soldiers, four singles and four of each number from two to seven). The banker puts four cards on a table in front of him, for example, a king and queen on top, and a knight and single on the bottom.

Now let us assume that one better puts his money on the queen, another one on the knight, and there are no other betters. The banker with his right hand draws the top card from the deck held in his left hand and puts it face up on the table. If the drawn cards do not match any of the four cards on the table, nobody wins but cards are drawn until one is matched. If a king is drawn first, the banker wins the bet placed on the queen, but nothing else, for the bet on the knight is covered only by a single for the banker; thus if a knight is drawn first before a single, the banker has to pay the better who has the knight but not the one who has the queen. The game appears to be fair, for the banker enjoys no advantage. Because of its simplicity, cheating and quarreling are unlikely. Although they are passionate card players, they are moderate drinkers, and the word *borracho* (drunkard) is the most contemptible one in their vocabulary.

Loreto was built in the first half of the last century and apparently was the seat of the shrine from the start, for the people believed even in those early days that it was a favorite spot of the Virgin Mary and chosen by her as one of the places to perform miracles.

The present church is of comparatively recent origin and the magnificent oil painting is a gift of Pope Gregory XVI. However, the church built in the last century which was in the immediate vicinity of the present one, was a much more splendid structure. It contained the figure of the Virgin Mary in pure hammered silver, with a golden crown on the head, and adorned with many precious stones and pearls. The rest of the jewels of the church were also of exquisite workmanship and great value, but at the turn of the century the place was attacked by pirates who slaughtered the priests and the population, set the church and other buildings on fire, and stole the silver Virgin and all the church jewels.

The old church was built of such durable materials, however, that it could resist even such vandalism. The walls are still intact, only the steeples collapsed and the roof caved in. We were curious to see this structure and upon visiting it found that the proper name of the Virgin here was "Our Virgin Mother, Mother of the Light." On the frontispiece of the church large carved letters read "*Nuestra Señora de la luz*" under a beautifully carved figure of Mary, surrounded by a halo, as she is saving a man from the clutches of Satan. Around her were numerous angels carved in bas-relief that would be worthy of note in any museum or art gallery.

In one of the church vaults we saw many skulls and human skeletons scattered around. We were informed that they were the remains of rich people who wished to be buried in the vault of the church in the belief that the continuous praying around them would somehow atone for the sins they had committed during their lifetime. They were sadly mistaken, however, for Jack Morgan and his fellow pirates broke open the vaults in the hope of finding treasures there, cast them out of their resting place, and then set the House of God on fire, so that no one could utter prayers for mercy within its walls anymore.

The walls are bare and the traces of fire still visible. The onetime magnificent altar is overgrown with weeds, but the huge stone tablet plastered in the wall behind it is intact and in its original position. This tablet is a bas-relief of remarkable beauty representing Mexico's best-known saints. The Virgin Mary stands at the top, to the right of her St. James rides on a turbaned infidel, to the left is St. John of Pomasan, with a landscape of a high waterfall in the background. In the second row, St. Francis Xavier baptizes Indians, with Indian huts and riders in the distant background. In the third or lower row are St. Joseph and St. Francis of Santa Fé, each standing on a terrestrial globe, extending hands to each other over the surrounding oceans.

Underneath the tablet two smaller white marble slabs of elliptical shape are visible. They have the following inscriptions:

A Devocion De Señor Dn.
Franco. Ant. Maria Dl.
Vallegova Nadori Capin
Gendes Te Reino

+

Ides Vesposa
Da Maria Ignacia
Martinez De
Ugarte Ano E 1761

Scattered around the peninsula we have often come across with valuable sculptures and paintings which were sent at one time from Spain and Rome to decorate churches and cloisters; sometimes the artists themselves were sent, who executed their masterpieces right here. In La Paz for example, an acquaintance, a very kind lady, is in the possession of a remarkably beautiful oil painting, unquestionably an original Murillo, a picture of a lady with a dagger in her heart. We have done our best to persuade her to sell us the painting, but in vain, for according to her it represents the "Virgin Santissima" and the curses of heaven would fall upon her, should she sell it for money, just as they fell upon Judas for selling Christ.

In the afternoon, cockfights, horse races, foot races, and other such spiritual exercises were held on nearby lawns. Without such amusements Spanish community life is unimaginable.

The evening we spent in the hospitable house of the padre, who is truly a cultured gentleman, and his two chaplains are also pleasant conversationalists. At dinner time the table was covered with a spotless white cloth, and the heavy silver dishes amply filled with a variety of wines and food, everything that this part of the peninsula is capable of producing.

After dinner, upon Padre Taori's suggestion—who by the way has the title of Dean and wears the red belt—we sat down to play whist at which our reverend father was an expert. They trounced us and were very pleased about it. The reverend fathers play whist differently, however, than the usual rules prescribe. They knew nothing about "robbers" and if one side scored eleven, they would win and a new game would be started. Furthermore, once when I and my partner scored a grand slam and four honors in addition, the padre obstinately insisted that the play did not count and we had to deal it over for the cards were not properly mixed.

The next morning we arrived at Comondor, a two-storied village. Our route led us through a valley and we passed by scattered small houses and huts all of which had small plantings and vegetable gardens. Water being scarce, cultivation of the soil is necessarily limited, for during the dry season not one drop of rain falls and all plantings have to be irrigated.

Comondor was built on high ground in the delta of a small mountain stream. This place is noteworthy not only for the advantages of its natural location and singular architecture, but for the bloody events that took place within its walls in the not too distant past. The building itself is a perfect square with two rows of gun turrets and as usual, accessible only through the top. The walls are made of adobe and are twelve feet thick. In addition, the structure is surrounded by a ten-by-ten-foot moat and the moat again is encircled with a wall sixteen feet high and twelve feet thick. This wall again is lined with a double row of pointed stakes.

This was the fortress in which the remnants of the army of the peninsula took refuge in 1847, pursued by the North American forces, and where 125 Mexican patriots resisted for more than four months the siege of about 1,000 North American soldiers who were equipped with cannons. Nevertheless, they were decimated by the nightly forays of the besieged. The bloody history of this siege and the ultimate capture of the fort (after five days of artillery barrage) prove the defensive value of thick adobe walls when they are in good hands. Not one of the sixteen-pound cannonballs was able to damage the walls even though they were fired from less than 200 paces. The Mexican snipers picked off the American artillerymen through the gunholes by their cannons. Few cannonballs penetrated deeper than one foot, most of them rolling off the walls into the ditch, hardly leaving more of an impression than a drop of ink on a blotter. This type of construction is quite unusual. It forms the kind of fortification not found in any military manual.

Leaving Commodor we travelled about ten miles, riding parallel to the ocean over rolling terrain covered in places with cedar and piñon trees but no greenery. After fording a small creek we got into a narrow mountain pass which rose continuously for some miles. Our trail was twisting and quite steep at times and, being covered with sharp stones, made our progress quite difficult. The surrounding mountains rose to a height of about 2,000 feet, and were composed mostly of hard slate, the sharp fragments of which made it particularly hard for our animals.

Reaching the highest point of the pass we descended again on the northern side and soon arrived at a wide valley where again we crossed a small stream. Here in some miserable huts we came upon about 100 wretched-looking Indians who seemed to be living solely by raising goats, as they had no cultivated gardens and no livestock could survive on the barren land where there not a blade of grass is visible for miles.

After crossing several similar mountains and mountain passes, toward evening we reached another valley where there were a few fruit orchards and vegetable gardens, as well as fields of corn. At one place we saw very nice peaches and the houses had chili peppers hanging all over them, as usual strung on long strings.

The valley became more and more interesting as we advanced, showing signs of prosperity in many places. The houses were larger and more attractive and alongside the road there were numerous vineyards fenced with cacti or adobe walls. In one of them we saw many pretty *doncellas* singing while picking peaches and grapes, and a great many

169

baskets were overflowing with luscious fruit, which greatly tempted our appetites, especially those carried on the heads of *doncellas* with their flashing black eyes. Naturally we could not just pass them by, so we rode over to the house and asked the young girls for some fruit. Some of them ran off, others just stared, but a few approached us with smiles, carrying clusters of grapes. At that moment a Cerberus-like head appeared in the window and roughly ordered the girls into the house, announcing that he himself would bring us the grapes. The angry master immediately brought as much fruit as we wanted to buy and could carry, and so we trotted on. Soon we came to a salt lake where we settled down for the night, though not willingly, but it was so dark by then, that we hardly could see one another.

We left our very uncomfortable camp, where neither water nor firewood was available, as soon as it was light enough, following the western shore of the salt lake. In a short time we entered the small village of San Carlos, which consisted of one, single-story adobe house. It had neither door nor window and had to be entered from the top by a ladder. Still, San Carlos can claim an architectural curiosity, for on top of the building a whitewashed, cone-shaped and peaked, ovenlike structure rose. We had no time to enter the house and discover the purpose of this peculiar structure, but Pilka maintained that these were ovens for bread baking, and the emerging smoke and vapor seemed to bear out his contention. We also noticed a band of cowherds who drove their cattle from the salt lake into the mountains and used slingshots for this purpose, slinging large pebbles mercilessly at the ears of the terrified animals with apparent success, for the poor, trembling, bellowing beasts were scurrying in the desired direction.

We bought some red onions in San Carlos, each of which weighed at least eight pounds, which should give the reader an idea about the fertility of the soil here.

Continuing our trip, we soon came to a place where the road forked. We followed the apparently more traveled one, but in a few miles it came to a dead end and we found ourselves in the midst of a huge cactus jungle and some isolated poplar trees. Not wanting to retrace our steps, we followed compass direction by slashing our way in a straight line towards Magdalena, where we arrived safely around noontime after a very tiring ride. But we did not reach the right road until we had almost arrived at the city. Our entire trip was over cactus-covered spaces, often crisscrossed with cattle tracks which served as trails, although they were at least one foot deep with sand. We had to choose between thorns and sand.

After La Paz, Santa Magdalena is the most important port of the peninsula, situated in a bay of the same name, which offers a spacious and safe anchorage. The bay is teaming with a variety of much-sought-after fishes, extraordinarily large numbers of oysters, crabs, and turtles. Pearl fishing flourishes on the nearby islands. Due to these circumstances the town carries on a thriving trade with the ports of Sonora and other ports of western Mexico, and in recent years the town's population has increased considerably and improved its quality of life. Brick and stone houses with attractive exteriors have taken the place of the old adobe houses. New streets lead in every direction, and already a few important international trading firms have settled here. Naturally, these have considerable influence on the welfare of the city and its environs. They put money into circulation, which enables the natives to sell their produce and from the profits purchase articles of comfort, which only a short time ago were completely unknown to them, but to which by now they have become so accustomed, that they are almost indispensable.

There is a spacious and well furnished French restaurant in town, whose table—to do honor to its owner—is amply provided with the products of the animal and plant life of the regions of the Purple Sea. In addition, Mr. Vebreau's wife is an exceptionally skilled cook, raised in Marseilles. She is well versed in the secrets of the French cuisine and can create something out of nothing or transform seemingly inedible material into the most appetizing morsels.

Santa Magdalena has a large plaza which, according to Mexican custom, is planted with trees of beautiful foliage, ornamented with a fountain in the center which, however, was dry during our stay there, for the pipes were clogged somewhere in the mountains.

There is no school in the town as yet, although it is well provided with churches and priests and it can also boast a monastery and a convent.

The foreign inhabitants, however, provided for the education of their children by importing from England an Episcopalian seminarist whom they pay well, and who instructs their children regularly not only in elementary subjects but in advanced studies as well. For this purpose, the English and Americans have equipped a separate build-

171

ing where children under twelve receive instruction in the morning and the older ones in the afternoon. The institute is well equipped with instruments to explain and teach natural history, geography, physics, and other sciences properly.

It is regrettable that the time at our disposal was so limited that we could not spend at least a couple of days in town and explore all the interesting things, especially the various fishing activities in the bay. The American consul, through whose kind offices we acquired all our information, states that no less than thirty-eight vessels fish in the bay, employing about 2,000 persons.

The consul also told us that the area between San Bartolome and Santa Magdalena is overrun by *ladrones* or bandits and that we should not count on completing our venture without any trouble. On his advice we requested the commander of the *quartel* or harbor fort to assign a military escort to us. The Commander, Don Hyacynto Ferrara, an artillery major, was kind enough to put six cavalry men immediately at our disposal, with whom we left town toward evening. Soon after we crossed the salt plain, Santa Magdalena disappeared on the horizon.

For a long while our route was over the salt plain, the surface of which was as hard and flat as a table top and on which the visibility was almost unlimited, although the shimmer of the salt was hard on the eyes.

Finally leaving the salt plain behind, we came into a region covered with artemisia and soon after we were in mountains where there was no sign of life beyond the much needed element we spurred on our mules. Soon we spotted smoke rising from this green area and although our way we have seen many large pieces of ammonites, different fragments of innoceramus and very large quantities of gleaming flakes of selenite (moonstone). We saw this mineral in many places, shining on distant mountain sides and tops. It appears in great abundance over an area of hundreds of miles.

For several hours we made fast progress but night was closing in without our finding any water. In the distance we saw a green spot and in the hope of finding the much needed element we spurred on our mules. Soon we spotted smoke rising from this green area and although we rushed as fast as we could, it was in vain, for the night descended suddenly, and darkness enveloped us so that we had to dismount and lead our animals. In a few minutes we reached the steep banks of an arroyo, where we had to stop as we could not see any further. A few of us descended and searched for water for several hundred paces all around without finding any. We were finally forced to pitch camp.

The escorting soldiers knew nothing of the region, for it was only a few weeks ago that they had come from Acapulco to their present station.

In the morning we realized the wisdom of the decision not to continue in the darkness. The arroyo in many places was as much as fifty feet deep and squeezed between almost vertical walls, while the bottom was covered with huge boulders. The trail was cut into the wall without rails, and it would have been a miracle had we not fallen to the depths in the darkness.

This must have been a frequent occurrence here for there are many crosses on both sides of the arroyo. These crosses have the peculiarity of having been erected not to mark the graves of the deceased, but to prevail on the passerby to pray for the soul of the donor. For example, there was a wide board nailed on top of one of the crosses with the following inscription: "Wanderer, pray for the soul of Donna Maria, who erected this cross in memory of her brother, murdered in this arroyo. A.D. 1853."

We pressed onward on a plain covered with artemisia and crisscrossed with sheep tracks, and in fact we have seen many large sheep herds. We came upon Indian shepherds whom we tried to persuade to sell us a few lambs, but we could not prevail upon them until an imposing-looking chief appeared who quickly arranged a trade.

After a ride of about ten miles we arrived at San Marcos.

In the midst of the plain, a sandstone hillock 500 feet high rises with almost vertical sides, crested on the top by San Marcos. The storms deposited sand on the north side of the rock, which through the years hardened and made it easier to climb that side up to a point; but further up, there were fissures and crevices in the hard rock and we had to climb between gaps made passable by an astounding achievement of labor. For instance in one place, between the vertical rock wall and the wall next to it which resembled a square tower, the Indians had positioned crosswise, wooden beams of immense size (how they managed it, only they can tell), on which at a height of about 100 feet they had placed horizontal planks in the shape of the spokes of a wheel and which rested on a vertical hub. These planks then spiraled in such a graduated rise that mules could ascend and descend easily even when burdened with weights of several hundred pounds.

On our way up to the town we kept meeting Indians coming down at a rapid pace with empty sacks. And we left behind others going up, carrying on their backs heavy *burros* (large bags of sheepskin or cowhide) filled with peaches, grapes, and other fruits. At last we reached the top, which is a completely flat plain with an area of about seventy-five acres. We stopped before an extensive and double-spired church of attractive exterior, from which streets radiated in all directions; the streets were filled with many square buildings the walls of which facing the plain had only small openings like gunholes, all doors being on the inside.

Every house was whitewashed and two-storied, the upper story recessed on account of the covered portico below. While the ground floor can be reached through the interior doors, the upper story is accessible only by ladders, as is the case with all such structures. From the roof of the first story wooden steps lead to the top which also separate the quarters of different families from each other. When we climbed to the top of one of these buildings, we found immense quantities of peaches split in two, spread to be dried in the sun.

We entered several houses and the inhabitants received us hospitably. At several places they laid in front of us round, flat baskets filled with some curious looking small cakes which they called *guayave* and which resembled somewhat the nest of the Hungarian yellow jacket. It has the color and thinness of a wafer. The lady of the house took a few of these into her hands and crumbled them into a finely woven flat basket and, following her example, we ate them out of our hands, much like children munching bread crumbs. We could not find out the details of how *guayave* is made, for it is kept as a great secret due to its popularity, but I believe it is made of sugar, eggs, and corn flour.

The families live on the first and second floors, mostly four to six to a house. The ground floor is used only for storage, and is well stocked with dried melons, maize, sweet potatoes, squash, beans, and numerous other foods, while the outsides of the houses are covered with strings of "chili colorados."

It seems the population is well provided with all the necessities, all grown in the vicinity; they appear to be well contented, for they are very quiet, peaceful, and hospitable with a joyous expression on their faces. As we were comming and going in the town, we watched them empty their *burros* and distribute the weight among themselves before climbing up the ladders. On these occasions they pointed to the mounds of peaches and grapes and with the words "*coma, coma caballero*" (eat, eat gentlemen), they encouraged us to take and eat as much as we liked.

They wear a black-and-white striped blanket for an upper garment, wide, baggy trousers to the knee, long, striped cotton stockings and leather boots. The women's pants are not quite as wide and are lined with some elastic fabric, as are their stockings, which give their legs a comical look, reminding one of elephant legs.

Apparently these people have very little contact with the Mexicans, for very few of them speak Spanish. This may be due to the fact that in the old days Spanish law prohibited Indians to leave their villages without permission, and whites were also forbidden to mingle with the Indians without a permit. (Murray, *Customs in the Spanish Colonies*, London, 1823.) All the same, they have a superficial and muddled concept of Catholic religion, for crucifixes, pictures of saints, and holy-water receptacles can be seen in their houses and, as I mentioned before, they have an attractive church with bell towers where an Indian officiates as a priest. Although he possesses guilded vestments and a bishop's miter, he has not the slightest acquaintance with the magic of reading and writing. It would be interesting to find out how he could read the mass from the missal. Perhaps he is of the opinion that good intentions are just as pleasing to the Almighty as good deeds. If that is the case, we willingly share his belief and wish him and his flock happiness and contentment.

Although we ascended to the town on muleback, we wanted to come down on foot, leading our animals before us. When we reached the plain, there were large numbers of cattle, mules, and horses scattered all over, but guarded by shepherds, and as it was late in the day we pitched our tents next to ditches dug by the Indians which contain ample and good water throughout the year.

Between our camp and the town there is a small stream in which water surfaces only for a distance of a few steps and then vanishes in the sand and flows for miles underground, as is the case with many rivers and creeks in California and Mexico. The distance from the ditches to town is almost a mile and one can readily imagine how difficult it is to carry water to the mountaintop, especially for people who do not have utensils suitable for that purpose. It is done now by using woven straw baskets and leather sacks.

As one looks up from our camp to the town situated on the flat top of the stone monolith, and views the whitewashed houses with their gun-hole windows, one is involuntarily reminded of European castles like Lilienfeld, Königstein, and Petervárad, but especially the castle of the Batthanyi family at Siklos, as viewed by the traveler from the road to Eszék.

For those acquainted with the history of the Spanish conquest, San Marcos is also reminiscent of the castles discovered by the armies of Cortez in the northern parts of Mexico, for example, Capistlan in the Guastepeque Mountains, which is described by J. G. Solis as follows: "The town is a natural fortress as it was built on top of a high and steep mountain to which access is very tiring and difficult and our soldiers could use their hands only for climbing, lest they slip down into the depth." The same author in his interesting work, *Conquista de Mejico, por Cortez* (Madrid, 1791, 3rd. ed.) mentions the siege by Cortez's army of another similar fortress. He states: "The Indians feigned confusion and disorder among their ranks in order to entice us to follow them into the steepest ravines. But we were wise to them, for we knew that had we done so, the Indians would have turned around and, amidst a terrific hub-bub, showered a barrage of rocks on us from the mountaintop, thus pounding our entire army to death. Therefore, our captain Diaz Bernard advanced with a few officers only to reconnoitre the situation, leaving the main force behind, for we never knew what the Indians planned, nor the dangers that threatened the army of His Most Catholic Majesty."

At ten-thirty at night, with a blinding flash, a meteor streaked across the sky from north to east, its horizontal course paralleling that of the earth. Its light was so intense that it overshadowed that of my lamp, by which I was writing in my tent. Five minutes later a distant roar that sounded like the echo of cannon fire could be clearly heard.

Our mules wandered all over, mingling with the ones from San Marcos and it took us a lot of running about to collect them, so it was nearly seven o'clock by the time we got on our way.

The trail for the first few miles led us in a northwesterly direction and steadily descended into a wide valley. Soon we found ourselves at a much lower elevation than we have been in the last few days. This plain we were on was below the region of the red sandstone of San Marcos on the sides of which the outlines of the earth layers were clearly visible, offering geologists an extremely rich harvest of valuable geologic specimens and undoubtedly important geologic discoveries. At places we came very close to the high banks which edged the valley, showing five clearly defined strata. The top layer was hard and dense sandstone like the monolith of San Marcos, then hard, whitish clay,

18. *San Marco on the California Peninsula*, original drawing by John Xántus, 1858;
print by Haske & Co., Pest, 1859

under which was deep red sandstone, layered above brownish-grey, sandy clay.

Although we had hardly advanced more than twenty miles since last night, the contour of the landscape changed completely. Crossing this second mesa the trail narrowed into a high mountain pass where we proceeded between vertical walls several hundred feet high; the flora changed to tall pines and cedars until these trees formed veritable forests. The few cacti and artemisia here were dwarfs and stunted as if they felt themselves to be in an alien land. Our trail vanished in many places and often we had to guess our path, but we met with no serious difficulties.

Finally about noon we struck a comparatively fresh cart track. Following it, I rode ahead to get a better view from a mountaintop, when from a distance of twenty-five paces I saw three grizzly bears in the middle of the track. Flattening myself on my mule, I was fortunate to be able to retrace my steps without attracting the monsters' notice, undoubtedly helped by the wind blowing away from the bears. My companions became quite excited when told about the kind of obstacles on our trail and, after a short council of war, I was delegated with the assistance of Pilka and Manuel to chase the bears while the others protected our animals.

Cautiously and holding our breath, with rifles at the ready, we advanced and and at the turn where I had previously seen the bears, we crouched behind a rock. Looking around very cautiously, I noticed the trimvirate in the same position as before. One of them was lying down and the other two were rolling in the sand. Pilka immediately took aim, but his gun misfired, then Manuel tried his luck, but his rifle would not fire either, and finally I aimed at one of them and *pfff*, only the fuse crackled.

The bears sat up on their haunches, pricked up their ears and, turning their heads in every direction, listened for a few seconds, then vanished into the pine bushes just as we primed our rifles for a new attack.

After calm consideration we realized how lucky we had been that our rifles had gotten wet during the night and misfired, because even we could not have expected to kill all three bears and the wounded ones would certainly have attacked us. Although the three of us were in fairly secure position, they could have wreaked destruction among our animals and possibly cost human lives.

The grizzly bear (*Ursus horribilis* Ord - Syn.: *Ursus ferox* Linne, Cuvier, Audobon and others) is unquestionably the most formidable of the wild beasts of North America, including the jaguar and panther. If it had the speed of the African lion or Asian tiger it would be even more dangerous, for it is stronger than the lion and as cruel and bloodthirsty as the tiger. Fortunately, it cannot overtake a horse otherwise its human victims would greatly increase, but it can easily overtake a man on foot, no matter how fast he runs. There are hundreds of authenticated cases proving the bloodthirsty bent of this fierce monster, and there are few hunters in western America who do not have at least a few stories to tell about encounters with the grizzly. Whenever we hear of such adventures we are easily persuaded that not a few human lives fell victims to a desperate struggle with these beasts.

The grizzly is an animal of huge proportions and weight. I shot one near Fort Tejon that weighed 1,200 pounds, and in the San Francisco zoo there is a live specimen called "General Scott" which is only five years old, but already weighs 1,550 pounds. I have seen and shot many that weighed about 1,000 pounds, so that we can safely state that the average weight of a fully developed specimen is about 900 pounds. On the whole, in size and weight the grizzly is similar to the polar bear. It is much stockier than black or white bears, the ears are much larger, the forelegs much thicker, and its appearance far more terrifying. The teeth are very strong and sharp; the fangs are long and spiky. But its paws are feared the most and with good reason for they are so huge that they leave footprints fifteen inches long and twelve inches wide. To top all this, long, bonelike, sharp claws, no less than six inches long protrude from them. Naturally, I am speaking of a fully grown specimen.

The crescent-shaped claws curl downward and would be even longer but for the fact that at least one inch is broken or worn off as the grizzly constantly scratches and digs the soil with its claws in search of weasels, rats, badgers and all kinds of sweet roots. At times it can dig up the ground to a surprising depth with its claws. All the same, its claws are sharp enough to strip the hides of horses, cattle, or buffalo in a few seconds, which seems to be its favorite occupation.

The grizzly's color is usually a deep red mixed with white and ash-grey hair, giving it a grey overall appearance. But it cannot be said that the gray coloring is a universal or exclusive characteristic of the species for there are some that are entirely white, yellow, red, or even black. The season and the climate unquestionably influence the color, although the length of the hair is always uniform and is much longer and thicker than that of other bears.

The eyes are remarkably small in proportion to the huge body. The eye itself is no larger than an ordinary musket ball and that part of it which is visible in the hairy slit is only as big as grape shot, but it shimmers and is watchful.

The habitat of the grizzly is along the huge mountain ranges of the Rocky Mountains and its branches, from the northern shores of the Arctic Ocean all the way to the mouth of the Rio Grande on the northwestern coast of the Gulf of Mexico.

It is not found in eastern Canada or east of the Mississippi in the United States. The reason for this is quite clear. Before colonization these territories were covered with limitless, dense forests and most of them still are today. The grizzly being a very awkward and clumsy tree-climber is seldom found in the great forests. The black bear usually climbs a tree, catches its prey there, and strangles it by pressing it against the tree. The grizzly on the other hand seldom climbs a tree on account of his claws. It might climb dwarfed trees, tangled bushes, or crooked tree trunks. Most of the time it is found among the inaccessible tangled brush which serves as a safe shelter, and in whose comfortable shade it waits for its prey while feeding on raspberry or other varieties of sweet berries.

The grizzly particularly likes to be in the vicinity of creeks and rivers where it can hunt among the willow bushes or jagged cliffs, and especially among prostrate juniper groves where no creature can follow it unless equipped with a hide as thick and hairy as its own.

It is an omnivorous animal. Fish, bird, frog, lizard, snake, fruit, or root equally satisfy its appetite. Insect grubs are a great favorite and they are in great abundance on the bottom parts of fallen trees. To reach them, it can roll away tree trunks so large that two oxen could not budge them.

At times it amuses itself by digging up the soil as pigs do, and often on a moonlit night it is capable of digging up several acres so completely that not a blade of grass remains. Like all other bears it likes sweets, wild strawberries, raspberries, blackberries, and will travel miles for them. Whenever it can it raids the beehives and is capable of consuming the honey of six to eight hives for supper.

Naturally it cannot catch a buffalo or deer in flight, but occasionally it manages to sneak up and capture them. Should it catch a panther or lynx as it feeds, it would snatch away the prey without further ado. It is known to have chased packs of hundreds of wolves, snatched their carrion to feed on, and remained until every bit was devoured.

Many times people have tried to tame two cubs but without success. Last year I too tried to tame two cubs that were hardly a month old when captured. For about six months they were so tame that they ate out of my hands, slept on a sheepskin in front of my door, and followed me around for miles like dogs, whether on foot or on horseback. After this period, however, they became irritable, started to attack the dogs with whom until then they had played amicably, and a few times they ran away into the mountains. I had to bring them back by force and in chains. Finally, it was impossible to come near them because they had become so vicious and so I was forced to shoot them.

For a long time the polar bear was considered the most dangerous of the species and many travelers' tales of adventure refer to them. People were told of hair-raising encounters that whalers and other travelers in the Arctic seas have had with them. But the fame of the polar bear will soon be overshadowed by the grizzly, which was almost unknown until now. Ever since the discovery of gold has lured half of the world's adventurers to California, the knowledge of the grizzly has begun to spread, for the valleys of the Sierra Nevada are the favorite habitat of this ferocious breed. Prospectors for gold came upon them many times in the mountains. Often only a desperate struggle determined who had possession of the land, and more than once the grizzly was the winner, even when confronted with large and fearless parties, experienced in fighting all kinds of wild beasts.

Hundreds of such adventures in recent times were reported in the California daily press and in the diaries of travelers. Some were exaggerated, most of them were true. These stories prepare the readers both here and in Europe to accept the grizzly as an equal to the elephant, the hippopotamus, or even the king of the animal kingdom, the lion.

A white hunter, no matter how skilled and experienced, will seldom attack it unless he rides an exceptionally good horse, his line of retreat is open, and most importantly, he has dependable weapons.

Indians generally avoid it with dread. Should an Indian be lucky to kill one, the event is considered an heroic deed by the entire tribe. The hero's rank is raised and the bear dance is performed for days in his honor.

I have often come upon a grizzly unexpectedly and must admit that I have always avoided it even though I am blessed with good eyesight and a steady hand with a rifle. In spite of this, I can claim to have shot no less than nine grizzlies during my stay in California, but in all fairness I must add that each one of them was brought down during a hunt organized for that purpose. While I was completely secure, the poor unsuspecting beast literally stepped in front of the barrel of my rifle, or as I lay in ambush at night in a favoring wind, the grizzly approached the bait we set out for it with complete confidence, expecting a leisurely meal. It often came so close that it almost collided with my gun. Not long ago I shot an exceptionally beautiful specimen which I prepared with great care and sent on its way to Hungary. Perhaps by the time these lines come off the press, it may be displayed in the collection of the National Museum and the reader may have the chance to see the grizzly as it is in reality. I believe that there is not one in our country so far and very few in all of Europe. I should like to state that the specimen sent to the National Museum is a female and only two years old; however the animal does not reach full maturity until the age of four.

After the encounter with the grizzly, we continued our trek and were soon in the cloud-covered Sierras. After a few miles we reached the shore of a creek which we wanted to cross without stopping, but our mules sank in the quicksand of the bed. By the time I noticed my animal sinking it was too late to spur it on and pull it out by the reins, so I jumped in the water and struggled across. The rest of the company did likewise, while only the backs of the mules were visible in the water. Relieved of their burden, however, they managed to scramble across without mishap and only the luggage got wet.

From there we reached a deep canyon with a gurgling, crystal-clear stream, which in a few hundred paces disappeared in the sand to reappear again further on. In the bed of the stream there were many small poplars which were densely intertwined with grapevines. The shiny green leaves were a joy to behold amid the monotonous coloring of the austere cliffs.

At some places we saw unusually large green stones which must have been disgorged from the bowels of the mountains by a violent upheaval, and were now piled in a picturesque heap on the mountaintops. The mountain walls here were crisscrossed with milky white, narrow layers of quartz, and wherever the least amount of soil collected in the crevices, long-eared cacti and bayonet palms sprouted.

At the mouth of the canyon we came to a couple of salt lakes whence a good wagon trail led us to San Gabriel, a four-storied village which we reached in the early afternoon.

There is nothing particularly noteworthy about San Gabriel. Its population is about 300. The natives have extensive garden plots in the nearby valley, where fruits—especially grapes—and garden vegetables are successfully raised. Around the gardens we noticed a few narrow-leaved oaks (*Quercus olivaeformis*), the only specimen during our trip on the peninsula.

In the immediate vicinity of the village there is a stream running between high banks, on which there is a mill. In spite of all the effort to collect water, during at least ten months of the year there is so little of it that the mill can hardly grind the miller's own maize with which to bake his daily bread. The mill, like all such structures on the peninsula, is of quite simple and awkward-looking construction. I have seen many such mills in Hungary and I shall briefly describe it.

A waterwheel is fitted on the lower end of a vertical shaft, the top end of which is on the mill platform and is fastened to the upper millstone which revolves on the lower millstone as the shaft rotates. On top of this machinery hangs a very large cowhide bag, the upper part of which is fitted with a square-shaped frame and is open. The lower part gradually narrows so that the whole thing resembles an irregular, inverted cone. The narrow end of the cone, in which of course there is a hole, is tied with a string to a trough placed right under it. One end of the trough is fastened to the cone, the other end or the mouth is kept in equilibrium by a long, horizontal pole, one end of which rests on a smaller vertical pole and the other on a diagonal pole which is securely fastened to the roof of the mill. The rotary motion of the wheel and the stones drives the entire structure. The maize placed in the cone-shaped bag pours into the trough and from there onto the stones. It trickles into another through the holes cut into the side of the lower millstone. The ground maize is no finer than coarse grout.

After an hour's rest we continued among pleasant surroundings and after riding a few miles our trail took a sudden turn from the north to due west. In a short while we were among mountains quite similar to those we saw yesterday. The forest consisted mostly of cedars and pines.

It was our firm intention to reach the village of San Felipe so we galloped whenever possible, but the trail became quite steep, and was blocked in many places by rocks, and quite sandy in other spots, so that we were several miles from our destination when night descended. We had to dismount and lead our mules. Fortunately we encountered no further obstacles this time, in fact it was lightning all evening and this natural light was no small help in reaching San Felipe by about ten o'clock where, thanks to the kindness of the population, we spent a pleasant night.

There was a wedding as we arrived and the alcalde immediately invited us to the fandango. When we got there, everyone was noisily celebrating, dancing alternately the *cuna* and the *bolero* and everyone was enjoying himself tremendously. The alcalde and his wife took the place of honor at one end of the room. The wife was armed with a black, square bottle containing *aguardiente* which certain honored guests were invited to sample. The band consisted of guitars, violins, and tambourines and they accompanied their music with improvised songs. Some of the songs were so clever that the audience burst into long and loud laughter in appreciation of the singers' wit.

At the fandango I made the acquaintance of Don Pedro de Bacca who is one of the owners of the neighboring silver mines. He informed me that the mines produce not only silver but large quantities of copper, iron, and *azogue*. I first thought that the word *azogue* meant mercury, but later I was informed that to the Mexican miner it means silver ore suitable for amalgamation, as chemical analysis proved that the specimen collected here contain no mercury at all. I expressed a desire to have a sample of these ores so Señor Bacca immediately offered to send a man to the mines for them. Since it was around midnight I asked him not to inconvenience himself, but he insisted stubbornly and sent off a peon on horseback for the samples.

It was six in the morning when the peon returned heavily loaded with silver ore, but was unable to bring copper and iron due to the lack of time. As it was, he rode close to forty miles in five hours, and those mines are a few miles further in the mountains. Señor Bacca called the ore *madre de la plata* (mother ore). I mention this because it is the first time I heard this expression. In other parts of the peninsula I heard it called *quixa*.

Señor Bacca also presented me with a truly beautiful jaguar skin. The animal was brought down near the mine only a few days ago, and this was a pleasant surprise, the more so because we have come across the traces of the animal many times during our voyage but never met one. In fact I have to admit with some regret that I have never seen this beautiful and most dangerous representative of the cat family in its free state.

This is not really surprising, for the jaguar is a comparatively rarely seen animal, partly because it roams only at night, and partly, and fortunately for the animal world, this horribly bloodthirsty creature is not too numerous.

The jaguar (*Felis onca* Linne) is tawny colored on its side, with small, uniform, star-shaped spots on its back and neck. The chest and belly are white, the whiskers grey. The average length including the almost three-foot-long tail is about nine feet. Its feet are comparatively short and its waist hollow, somewhat like that of a horse.

It is a solitary animal and whenever civilization approaches, it deliberately withdraws. Although, like the peccary, it is completely fearless and charges its enemies without restraint, regardless of the number. It attacks not only to satisfy its hunger but also for the pleasure of blood-letting. When it charges a herd of cattle or a stud of horses, it will kill as many as it can, even though half a calf is enough for its meal.

The fact that it is the most skillful tree climber of all the bloodthirsty animals makes it all the more dangerous. Don Bacca claims that it can climb a tree with great speed with the help of its claws alone and that he often heard the clatter of the jaguar's claws while running fast from a distance of more than half a mile. According to him the jaguar can climb down a tree just as fast as it goes up.

The only live specimen I ever saw is the one in the Regents Park Zoo in London, and it is a miserable-looking one. It is common knowledge that it is blind in both eyes, which gives but a poor idea of the size and beauty of this animal in its free state. But since the London specimen is the only living one in Europe it is worth seeing.

The jaguar usually hides among the outer branches of a tree, lying there in ambush, especially near lakes and streams. As unsuspecting animals pass underneath, it jumps on them with lightning speed, sinks its sharp claws into their necks, and in a matter of minutes tears them apart.*

*Some years ago a Hungarian compatriot wrote a book about his travels in North America, which contains much valuable and correct statistical information, but also among other improbable claims, the author states that he participated in a jaguar hunt and shot one somewhere in the state of Wisconsin (if I remember correctly in the vicinity of Belleview or under 46° northern latitude) Such claim is on a par with

Its geographic location is very extensive for it is to be found everywhere from Paraguay to Northern Mexico and even in the southern regions of California. It turns up occasionally in the brush on the edge of the Gulf of Mexico in Texas. No jaguar was ever found above the 33rd degree of northern latitude, which is an established fact, and it is ridiculous for some European travelers to claim that they have shot jaguars around St. Louis, Kentucky, or Iowa. Not being versed in the natural sciences, perhaps without any intent to brag or mislead, they probably saw and shot a lynx or a panther, but their hunting area was at least 1,000 miles away from the nearest habitat of the jaguar.

Many travelers claim to have heard the roar of the jaguar in the forests and mountains, but those whose misfortune it is to live near their habitat have never heard it and know nothing about such tales. According to Señor Bacca screeching sounds are often heard in the Sierras, especially at night, but they come from other animals, mostly owls, for the jaguar never shrieks or roars, and the only sound it can utter and often does is a low, dull, sad growl.

Taking leave of our kind and hospitable hosts and with many good wishes from the simple but good people, we started on our way at seven in the morning. This was to be the last day of our journey for, although San Bartolome was nearly fifty miles away, we decided to make it in one day.

Before continuing our trip we decided to dispense with the services of the soldiers escorting us, for we realized that they were not needed at all as there was no sign of *ladrones* anywhere, and their presence was a burden on us and a hardship for them. When we made our intention known, the sergeant declared that it was not possible for them to return until we had reached our destination. They were under strict orders from the major to escort us to our destination or suffer the severest penalty. This being the case, a testimonial letter was written, signed by all of us, in which we stated that they have accompanied us to San Bartolome and we commended them for their faithful and courageous services.

After about six miles we arrived at the village of Quiarra where the road forked: one to the northwest toward San Diego, and the other

shooting giraffes or lions on the plains of Hortobagy. It would be less incredible if my distinguished compatriot had stated that he brought down a polar bear, for to be sure, Wisconsin is closer to that animal than to the jaguar. [This sarcastic comment by Xántus refers to Haraszthy's book, *Travels in North America* (Pest, 1844). Ed.]

to the southwest to San Bartolome. Both of them were good wagon trails, at least in the vicinity of the village.

Quiarra consists of many small, square, one-storied houses which as usual can only be entered by ladders. On the north side of the village the ruins of a large church can be seen, the walls of which were built of four-square-inch red sandstones. The exterior of the walls is smooth, in many places resembling polished marble. Around the building are the remnants of many houses, most of them already buried in the sand, although the walls of the church are nearly sixty feet high and mostly intact. The base of the building is in the shape of a cross with a square on the corners of the protruding sides, for what purpose we could not even guess, nor do we know who built it, what kind of a city it was, or who were the people who destroyed it.

As we were looking at the ruins, a native Mexican wrapped in a cape approached us mysteriously and addressed the following words to me: "I would like to tell you something, Sir, but to you alone and in private." I immediately followed him to his house where I found a number of women. For awhile I sat on a bench talking about indifferent subjects with him, awaiting with curiosity the disclosure of his secret. But it seemed that my friend was not pleased with the presence of the women and so he said nothing until I took my hat in hand ready to leave, when he begged me to stay. I then questioned him about the geography of the area and particularly about the ruins of the famous Rosario ruins which he claimed were identical with the ruins of Quiarra.

Finally I told him that I could not stay any longer as we were in a hurry to get to San Bartolome, upon which he again begged me to meet him at the roadside in a cedar grove near the edge of the village. As our caravan reached the grove, our man was already there, waiting. Lagging behind, I asked him to make his story short as we were in a hurry. He then told me that he had discovered a fabulously rich gold and silver mine. I asked him why did he not remove some of the treasure from his discovery. "Oh," he exclaimed, "it is obvious that you have not been long in this country, Sir, and you don't know that poor people cannot acquire wealth here. The rich would immediately rob me of it. But if you would take me under your protection, it would be a different story. Nobody would dare to deprive me of the fruit of my labor." Then he added: "My name is José Lacero, Quiarrai Jose Lucero, and please write it down so you will not forget it, and you can ask anyone in San Bartolome and they will tell you that I am an honest man." Of course I put his name in my wallet and galloped after my company. If any of my readers feels inclined to hunt for treasures, he will know where to look for the riches of Quiarra.

We continued amidst mountains of barren, red sandstone, without a trace of vegetation except some cacti.

We saw thousands and thousands of ground squirrels sitting on their haunches or running around on the mountainside and when approached they made yelping noises like small puppies. We tried hard to figure out how and on what these animals lived in these mountains, but we could not explain the secret of this unfathomable natural phenomenon. Their scientific name is *Spermiophylus Beechey* and they are found in large numbers along the seacoast from southern Mexico all the way to Oregon, to the great annoyance of gardeners, for they are just as destructive as their Hungarian cousins.

Around noon we rested and attended to our animals in a tiny one-story village named Abojo. Around this village we saw numerous and extensive ruins, very similar to the ones at Quiarra, also the ruins of an almost identical church. On one side several windows with pointed tops, somewhat in Gothic style, are still visible.

Gregg, in his recently published and highly interesting work based on voluminous research, states, that on all such ruins the remains of the Spanish coat of arms can still be detected and from this he quite naturally concludes that these structures were erected during the Spanish conquest and certainly supervised by Spanish priests. (*Anahuac and Ancient Aztec Remains*, by J. Gregg, L.L.D. Philadelphia, 1854.) Bearing all this in mind, whenever time permitted, I scrupulously searched for such emblems, but nowhere did I find even a trace of them. I inquired from intelligent natives but I did not find one who ever saw or heard of them.

The results of my inquiries so much contradicted Gregg's claims that as soon as I returned to Tejon, I obtained at considerable expense, the works of those distinguished Spanish historians who dealt with the ancient conditions of this land. Disregarding time and effort, I went through the numerous volumes of Antonio de Solis y Rivadeneyra, Miguel de Vanegas, Francisco Javier Clavijero and Marcos de Nizza and those of my readers who are interested in archeology will find the result of my findings in the following lines.

According to Vanegas, in 1538 a monk named Marcos discovered a large city with seven-story houses. In 1542 Francisco Vasquez de

Coronado reached the Gila River with his army. He continued southwest to the famous cities of Abo and Quivira. In other words, he went from the kingdom of Tigue to the land named Cibolo, which was ruled at that time by King Pattarax, where the wealth of the populace consisted mostly of black bulls (*el toros negros*), which provided them with food, clothing, and furniture. It seems to me that this proves beyond a doubt not only that Abojo and Quiarra are of Indian origin but also that buffaloes were raised there.*

The famous kingdom of Cibolo**, although very far from Mexico City, was nevertheless known to Montezuma, for there were many buffaloes in his zoo, to the great astonishment of Cortez and the Spanish nobles when they conquered the city. Vanegas claims that there were no buffaloes in Sonora or Chihuahua, nor even in the environment of the Gila and Colorado Rivers.*** As I mentioned before, today buffalo is only found on the prairies, and Vanegas and Solis maintain that since these animals do not inhabit California and Mexico, they had to be acquired from the neighboring lands. It is also well known that it was the custom in ancient Mexico to name people after their heroic deeds,† and cities were named after objects connected with their origin, thus commemorating them for posterity.‡

Summing up the data from the aforementioned authors, it is very probable that the kingdom of Cibolo meant the land where the buffalo comes from.

I would like to compare the architecture of the Aztecs with that of the peninsula. At Rosario and San Vicente there are seven-story buildings still in good and habitable condition; as the reader knows from my

---

*It is a well known fact today that there is no buffalo to be found west of longitude 108°.

**Today the word *Cibolo* means buffalo in the language of the Indians of New Mexico.

***The same author describes the buffalo as follows: "The Mexican bull (one of the rarest in this land) has a shaggy back like the camel, the sides are bare, the tail long, and a long mane hangs down from the neck like the lion's. The hoof is like the ordinary cattle's, the head is armed with horns like a bull's, and in fact it is just like a bull from the standpoint of ferocity, strength, and agility.

†For example the famous chief of Tezcucan—Nazahual Cayotel (hungry wolf) was so named because he slaughtered a whole pack of hungry wolves.

‡Mexico City's original name was Tenochtitlan (Cactus on the mountaintop). During the wandering of the Aztecs they observed a huge cactus standing by itself on top of a mountain, just as an eagle alighted on it. They considered this a good omen and built a city there. (Prescott: *Conquest of Mexico*, vol. I.)

descriptions, there are buildings of two, three, and four stories in many places, some built of adobe, some of stone, and others of the mixture of the two. According to Vanegas, there were seven-story structures in Quivira and Abo, and multistoried ones in Tagique. Moreover, the traces of extensive irrigation ditches are still visible in many places.

It is evident that ancient Mexicans as well as their neighbors built multistoried residences, whereas the Spaniards always built single-story buildings and very rarely a two-story one. Solis states that the city of Ixtacpalpa consisted of numerous two-, three-, and four-story houses, and that in Mexico City, the king's general resided on the third floor of the Zoo building. He further states that he saw a long wall stretching from the distant mountains all the way to the center of the city, next to which there were two stone-lined canals, so that when one was being cleaned, the other one was pressed into service. He goes on to say: "Two or three lines of conduits made of hollowed trees supported by stone and limestone columns every few feet, rest on the walls."

The ruins at Abojo, Quiarra, and numerous other places (the California peninsula, New Mexico, the northern parts of Mexico) undoubtedly were built centuries ago by Indians, even if we allow that a few were constructed under the guidance of Spanish missionaries after the conquest. Many references are made in the history of the conquest to individuals like Father Kino, for example, who penetrated distant Indian lands armed only with the cross and converted them. Under the influence of his religious fervor, he had churches and cloisters built by them. Among others, Vanegas mentions Father Juan Padella who at the head of a small army visited the northern part of the peninsula, which at that time was thought to be an island. Within a few days, however, his soldiers scattered in search of gold, for to use the author's expression "they were more interested in the acquisition of treasures than in converting and teaching crafts to the Indians." The saintly father was left all alone, but later he became the head of a large community, of which however there is no trace.

There are many noteworthy facts to be learned from Clavijero's interesting work which tend to confirm if not the identity, certainly the very close relationship between the aborigines of the peninsula and the Anahue people. He asserts among other things: "During their wanderings the Anahues built spacious houses in many places which they occupied for a number of years. The traces of their structures are still visible here and there especially around the Gila River, Pimeria and Zacatecas." Elsewhere, writing about the Aztecs, he states:

After crossing the Red River (Rio Colorado) about at 34° latitude and moving south and southwest they stopped at the great water (Purple Sea²) where they spent some time, and the ruins of their magnificent buildings can be still seen on both shores of the water. From there they moved south–southeast, and at 29° of northern latitude, they settled down once again on an island which is about 200 leagues northwest from Mexico City. This settlement today is known as Casa Grande for the remarkable size of the buildings on it, the ruins of which are still standing and which according to word of mouth legacy among the Mexican people were built by the Aztecs during their wanderings. All these *Casa Grande* were built in total conformity to the buildings found around the environment of Mexico City, that is they are all of 3 to 4 stories with a terrace on top and cannot be entered through the ground floor. The door is on the first, but most of the time on the second story so that it is inaccessible without a ladder. The probable purpose of this architecture was defensive. At night the ladders were pulled up so that only residents could enter and hostile elements kept out. On top of the *Casa Grandes* in many places there are additional elevations which according to legend were in the shape of towers. We do not know their exact purpose, but it is reasonable to assume that guards were posted in the towers to observe an enemy approach and give timely warning to the warriors to prepare the defense.

Reading this reminded us at once of Quiarra and Abojo, and perhaps the buildings there were meant to be *Casa Grande*.

Since the kingdom of Cibolo was mentioned, I find it necessary to quote from Clavijero that this kingdom consisted of seven cities, which reminds us once again of the Aztecs who were also formed of seven nations and whose structure was kept intact throughout their wanderings.*

And now let us try to find the location of the kingdom of Cibolo. At the present time there are two places on the California peninsula the names of which resemble Cibolo. One is Cibolletta and the other is La Joya de Ciboleta. The first one is 240 miles southwest of the Colorado River, while the second one lies—as our readers know—in

*The seven nations were: Xohimilca, Tepaneca, Chalcez, Hahinca, Flascala, Colhua, and Mexico. (Prescott: *Conquest of Mexico*, vol. II.)

191

the vicinity of San Bartolome, about 285 miles from the same river and in the same general direction. Vanegas asserts that Vasquez de Coronado advanced from the neighborhood of Zacatecas towards Tigue, which was built next to a great river, and there he first heard of the location of Quivira, one of the largest cities in Cibolo. Coronado immediately dispatched an army which moving southward about 100 leagues, reached Quivira without any difficulty, as the route is not too mountainous.

Considering that the Colorado is the only "large river" in this region, it seems evident that the city of Tigue reached by Coronado's army was on this river, and therefore that the Colorado River is actually about 100 leagues distant from the present day village of Quiarra. The mountains between the river and village are so insignificant that the valleys could qualify for plains; one can no longer doubt that the ruins of Quiarra were once the city of Quivira, and that Cibbolletta, La Joya de Ciboleta, Abojo, Quiarra, San Marco, Rosario and San Vicente were the famous seven cities of the kingdom of Cibolo. The comparatively flat landscape between the Colorado and Quiarra made it perfectly possible for buffalos to reach the latter, or at least a small herd could have wandered there and later could have been tamed. There are enough of such examples even today among the Choctaw, Cherokee, and other Indians.

The remainder of our journey from Quiarra was uneventful. We arrived safely in San Bartolome late in the evening, and the same night yet left *terra firma*. From the back of our mules we transferred onto the waves or rather the fragile, rolling, and pitching deck of the cutter, and the next morning on May 25 we were on the high seas sailing north.

A Note by John Hunfalvy*

In Hungarian literature there has been very little written so far about American antiquity and that is why I consider it important to add to Xántus' data. The research of historians like Clavijero (*Historia anti-qua de Mexico*) and many others proved the contention that in the sixth, twelfth and thirteenth centuries there were mass migrations in Central America, just as in Asia and Europe in the same period. The American migration headed toward Mexico from the north and two nations in particular, the Toltec and the Aztec, were participants. Both were warlike, agriculturist and highly civilized. The Toltec appeared around 648 in Anahuac, north of the valley of Mexico and planted the seeds of civilization among the primitive natives. They established agriculture, built cities and amazing pyramids; they painted hiero-glyphics, smelted ores, honed and carved the hardest stones, and or-ganized a well-regulated state structure. The original home of the Tol-tec was Huehuetpatlan, of which only the name is known, and it has become the object of research north of the Gila River. Driven from their homeland, the Toltec advanced slowly, planting and harvesting maize, raising cotton and building cities. It took them 100 years of wandering to reach their new home, Anahuac, where they built the city of Tula. Their advanced culture is evident by their ability to calcu-late time based on astronomical observations which were so precise that they knew the exact length of the year and the calendar even took into account the leap years. In the middle of the eleventh century, however, due to crop failures and famine, a devastating epidemic de-cimated them, and only a remaining few fled to the east and south where they again spread their highly developed culture. Tula was already in ruins at the time of Cortez. In Guatemala and the Yucatan peninsula, in the vicinity of Palenque and Mitla, there are ruins co-vered with wonderful paintings indicating a highly advanced civiliza-tion. On the Yucatan peninsula, especially around Valladolid, Merida and Campeche, mostly in the western part of the land, are the rem-

*Eminent Hungarian ethnologist, editor of Xántus's *Travels in Southern Califor-nia*.

nants of ancient buildings. East of Yucatan, on the island of Cozumel, there are also antique structures which were admired by the Spaniards as early as 1518 and 1519. Yucatan's most notable ruins are: *Casa del Gobernador* (Governor's Mansion) at Uxmal; *Teocalis* (God's chairs), and the arched vaults near Kabah; the ruins at Labnah with their domed columns; the almost Doric columns of the ruins near Zayi; the beautifully ornamented columnar walls of the ruins at Chichen. An ancient manuscript in the Mayan language, edited by a baptized Indian, enumerates the various seasons of the fifty-two-year period of Toltec occupation of some areas of Yucatan. The manuscript is in the possession of Don Juan Pío Perez, who calculates from the available data that the structures at Chichen originated in the fourth century and the ones at Uxmal in the middle of the tenth century.

After the decline of the Toltec empire, new tribes from the northwest moved into Mexico and occupied the land of Anahuac. Around 1170, the primitive Chichimec and later the seven armies of the Nahuatlac appeared. To these latter belonged the Aztec, who reached Tula in 1196 and the valley of Mexico in 1216, where around 1325 they built on one of the islands of the lake, Tenochtitlan or the city of Mexico. During their migration, the Aztec also have settled for lengthy periods at some places where they constructed stone buildings, the remnants of which are still being discovered. The search for the original Aztec homeland of Teo-Acolhuacan or Aztlan is also centered north of the Gila River. Many are of the opinion that the civilization found by the Spaniards in Mexico and other American countries is of Asian origin.

In the Toltec and Aztec architectural remnants and ruins there is perhaps some resemblance to the East Asian and Indonesian Islands' Buddha images. Joseph de Guignes (1759–1845), a French traveler in China, Indonesia, and the Philippines, concluded from a poorly explained passage of a Chinese author that the Chinese had visited America as early as 458. Silas Burrows, editor of the *San Francisco Herald*, is certain that the Japanese occupied Queen Charlotte Island and had contacts with the northern coast of America. Alexander von Humboldt (1769–1859), the eminent German naturalist, discoverer of isothermal lines and author of *Kosmos* (1845–1862), also states that the East Asians' ancient communication with western America is more than probable, and that the Asians most likely reached America's western shores between 55° and 65° of northern latitude, from whence they slowly spread their higher civilization southward. According to Francisco Lopez de Gomara (1510–1560), the Spanish historian and author of the early history of America—generally considered unreliable—ruins of ships from Cathay or China and Japan had been found on the northern coast of Dorado, in Quivera and Cibola in the sixteenth century. All these, however, are merely assumptions. An impenetrable haze covers the ancient history of the Toltec and Aztec. The devastation caused by the Spanish conquest and especially the strenuous efforts of the first bishop of Mexico, Zumaragga, and later, in 1641, those of the newly appointed bishop Don Juan de Palafox y Mendoza, to convert the Indians, to say nothing of their blind religious fanaticism, were responsible for the destruction of the records of Mexico's ancient history.

Now, only decaying, crumbling buildings, broken crockery, tools, waterpipes, ruins of roadways in large areas in both North and South America proclaim that here, too, a cultured, historic nation lived at one time. In 1773, two Spanish priests, Garces and Font, rediscovered on the southern shores of the Gila River the ruins of a large Aztec city where the huge Casa Grande de Montezuma still stood. Among natives of New Mexico there were rumors about the existence of a faraway ancient Aztec city called Grande Quivira. In the sixteenth century a Franciscan friar told many tales about the immense treasures in the land of Quivira and the gold-greedy Spaniards who were constantly searching for them. When they finally became convinced that such tales were all fabrications, they began to doubt the very existence of Quivira. But Vasquez de Coronado, the sixteenth century Spanish governor, actually advanced with a detachment of soldiers toward Quivira. From his report to Emperor Charles V, as well as from the story of his companion, Castañeda de Nageras, it seems that no treasures were found there, nor do they remember any large buildings.

After this, the Spaniards apparently gave up on Quivira. Only in the most recent times were new facts reported about this famous city. From a letter dated June 15, 1853, addressed to the Maryland Historical Society, Colonel Miles wrote from Fort Fillmore that Lieutenant James W. Abert, a graduate of the U.S. Military Academy (1831) who explored New Mexico in 1846–47, was the only officer who saw Grande Quivira. He first reached the abandoned village of Abo—northern latitude 34°25' and western longitude 106°. From there, covering fourteen miles eastward, he reached Quivira. Miles further reported that

Albert H. Campbell of Virginia, a railroad engineer who later surveyed the route through New Mexico and Arizona, visited Quivira twice, in 1830 and again in 1842.

According to Campbell, Quivira is located on a mesa (plateau) on the northwestern peak of the Sacramento Mountains. It appeared to be a large, densely populated and well-built city with well arranged, rectangular streets; at least three miles long (northeast to southwest) and one-and-one-half miles wide. Some of the houses were still standing and were of carved stone. (This completely contradicts Coronado's report which states that there were only straw houses in Quivira.) Two large buildings in particular caught Campbell's attention, one of which he thought was a church and the other a palace. In the building that he thought was a church, he was hoping to find treasures. After clearing away the débris he broke through the flooring under which he found an empty room, sixteen to eighteen square feet in size, whose scrubbed walls were covered with paintings or colored figures. In another place he found a cavern dug out of the rock and sealed with a carved stone slab. There was a corpse in the cavern which crumbled into dust as soon as it was brought into the open air. Digging further, he found four additional graves with corpses. Some distance from the city, Campbell stumbled on the opening of a cave, which he entered, and came upon a mine shaft in which he found traces of glittering ore. At the end of the tunnel there was a small chamber in which there were a crowbar, a chisel, a hammer or axe made of a black metal, not iron, and unusual crockery.

Returning to the town, he found on the west side an oblong water basin 150 yards long, 80 yards wide, and 50 feet deep. The bottom of the basin was paved and the sides lined with hewn stone. On the most southern end there was a large multistory stone building, on the corner of which were longish openings and small doors, presumably for the protection of the water cistern. The vicinity of Quivira is a treeless and waterless desert for miles and miles. On the northern end of the basin there were water conduits. Campbell rode forty English miles alongside of them in a northwesterly direction towards the White Mountains. This conduit is 12 feet wide and 10 feet deep, but it is dry now, because its opening is blocked by débris and the creek which at one time flowed into the cistern now flows into the Pecos River. The cistern in its entire length is lined with small hewn stones (not brick) on the sides as well as the bottom.

Starting from Quivira, a 100-foot-wide, paved highway leads to the east. Presumably Campbell followed this road for forty miles, and he believes that it led to Texas and Nacogdoches. About twenty miles from Quivira, on the northern side of this highway, Campbell came upon a large village built of stone where, as in Quivira, he found many painted pots and crockery. Miles communicated this information in his letter to Silas Burrows, editor of the *San Francisco Herald*, who published it in the August 15, 1853, issue of the paper; it was also sent to Alexander Humboldt.

Finally there was a letter published in the June 23, 1853 issue of the *Placerville Herald* of the San Bernardino valley about an ancient pyramid discovered in the Great Colorado desert. According to this letter, a party of five men followed the Colorado upstream about 200 miles from its junction with the Gila River, hoping to find a western tributary of the Colorado which would provide an easier and faster route over the desert to California. They found only barren and desolate desert on both sides of the river, but in the middle of the forlorn desert they found a huge pyramid, the top of which was already crumbling. This pyramid had supposedly fifty-two layers of stone and each layer was two feet thick, so that the entire pyramid was at least 104 feet high. Furthermore, the base of the pyramid was buried in the sand; they could not ascertain its depth, for they would have had to dig too deeply. They found other clues, too, from which they concluded that the barren desert of the Colorado was at one time America's garden, granary, and the residence of millions of people.

Until then, the belief was that the Aztec migration could be traced only as far as the Gila River in the north, but the discoveries at Quivira, and the alleged existence of ancient structures on the north bank of the Colorado greatly expanded the indications of the Aztec migration. However, the data supplied by American sources are so vague that one cannot build on them. Lieutenant Albert claims only that he saw Quivira, but has nothing to say on what he found there. Campbell describes his discoveries in greater detail, but if his facts are correct, his Quivira cannot be the same as the one reported in the ancient Spanish records, and it does not seem to be identical with Xántus's Quiarra, which was a village consisting of "numerous small houses" and on "the northern side of which were the extensive ruins of a large church." Around this church "the remnants of many houses are visible, but most of them are buried in the sand." Xántus found similar ruins near the village of Abojo. Lieutenant Albert mentions Abo, but calls it an abandoned village and makes no mention of any nearby ruins. Campbell talks only about Quivira. There, he found and saw much more than Xántus, but about the village of Abo or Abojo he is silent. Yet had he been there, he surely would have searched for treasures there also. What seems significant from Xántus's report, is the cross-shaped structure of the churches at Quiarra and Abojo, for if that is so than it almost certain that they were built after the Spanish conquest and under Christian influence and could not have had Aztec origin.

John Hunfalvy.

To Hungarian Scientific Institutions, Museums, Industrial or Agricultural Organizations and Individual Scientists

The Smithsonian Institute of Washington was founded for the sole purpose of spreading and disseminating knowledge among all peoples, and to promote this, it has made contact with similar institutions and individuals in every part of the world. It never failed to invite Hungarian scholars to join this endeavor. It is with regret however that the Institute states that so far its invitations have met with scant result, for only two Hungarian scientific societies have established contact with it: The Hungarian Scientific Institute and the University Library of Pest, and of these only the first offered an exchange of literary works, and thus little information was gained about scientific research in Hungary.

For this reason the Smithsonian is glad to take this opportunity once again to call the attention of Hungarian scholars to its purpose and wishes particularly to state the following:

1. The Institute will accept any book, periodical or chronicle in any language and from any individual or society, and offers in exchange American literary works of the same line of inquiry.

2. The Institute will exchange specimens of natural history for American ones, which may be specified by the sender.

3. If individual scientists wish to establish contact with Americans in the same field of research, the Institute will facilitate correspondence between them, and for this reason should Hungarian scientists or writers wish to circulate their books or papers among Americans in the same field, they could do so through the Institute and also receive the works of their American counterparts.

4. If desired the Institute will send American plants, drawings of machinery, or designs of public buildings and expects to receive in return similar articles.

5. All shipments to the Institute are to be sent to: Smithsonian Institution, Washington, North America, care of F. Flugel, American Consul, Leipzig (Saxony).

6. The sender's name and the content should be indicated on the package.

7. The cost of transportation between the sender and Leipzig is to be covered by the Hungarian party and between Leipzig and Washington by the Institute.

8. The Institute corresponds in English, but accepts and considers letters in all civilized languages.

The Academy of Natural Sciences of Philadelphia, wishes to call to the attention of sister institutes in Hungary, that it will accept all works, dissertations, periodicals, or yearbooks on the natural sciences and in return would offer its own yearbooks and periodicals as well as works of American scientists.

The Academy will accept specimens of all naturalia and will submit in exchange specimens designated by the donor.

The Academy calls particular attention to its world-famous skull collection, and it offers American Indian skulls for Szekler, Jasz, Kun, or other Magyar racial skulls. A brief commentary with each specimen is requested.

Address: Academy of Natural Sciences of Philadelphia, Philadelphia, North America.

Small packages may be forwarded through the Smithsonian Institute.

John Leconte requests Hungarian and Asian small mammals (stuffed or in alcohol) in exchange for North American specimens. (Address: Major J. Leconte, Philadelphia.)

Spencer Baird wishes Hungarian vertebrates for North Americans. (Address: Spencer F. Baird, Washington.)

Dr. Joseph Leidy asks for petrified Hungarian vertebrates. Offers North Americans. (Address: Joseph Leidy, M.D. Philadelphia.)

Dr. Edward Hallowell offers American reptiles for Hungarian ones. (Address: Edward Hallowell, M.D. Philadelphia.)

Edward Hitchcock would exchange American ore specimens for Hungarian ones. (Address: Edward Hitchcock, Esq. Boston.)

Dr. Thomas Brewer, requests Hungarian bird eggs and nests in exchange for American. (Address: Dr. Thomas Brewer, Boston.)

J. G. Torrey wants Hungarian plants for American plants. (Address: Professor J. G. Torrey, Amherst College, Boston.)

Dr. J. G. Leconte exchanges American insects for Hungarian ones. (Address: Dr. J. G. Leconte, 1325 Spruce Street, Philadelphia.)

G. Haldmann, wishes Hungarian insects for American ones. (Address: Professor G. Haldmann, New York.)

Dr. William A. Hammond would send American spiders and scorpions in exchange for Hungarian ones. (Address: Dr. William A. Hammond, corner 19th and Pine Sts., Philadelphia.)

John Cassin offers North and South American birds for Hungarian ones. (Address: John Cassin, Esq., care of Academy of Natural Sciences of Philadelphia.)

Commissioned by the above Institute and parties,

John Xántus

Editor's Postscript

Xántus on the Issue of Slavery and the Civil War

The period 1852 to 1856 during which Xántus surveyed and explored the Kansas and Nebraska territories were years of gestation for the bloody conflict of the Civil War. The region was the storm center in the struggle for supremacy between pro- and antislavery forces and this issue was further complicated by the dispute about the location of the transcontinental railroad route. The Kansas-Nebraska Bill of 1854 vainly attempted a compromise between the contending forces. When the attempt to organize the territory into statehood bogged down in bitter strife, the state became the site of bloody hit-and-run forays (John Brown's raid, and so on) and guerilla warfare terrorized the land, earning it the sobriquet, "bleeding Kansas."

It is noteworthy and puzzling that Xántus, who was a member of several railroad survey parties, and moreover had been a member of the U.S. armed forces, who had crisscrossed the country and was certainly well aware of the burning issues of the day, makes no mention of it in his *Letters*. In his diary and narratives, he freely discusses most other aspects of the American scene, yet he scrupulously avoids the slightest reference to conflicts over the question of slavery. Later, while in Washington during the early years of the war, he never speaks of his political leanings.

A plausible explanation is of course his isolation in the wilds of Indian territory and later at Fort Tejon and Baja California. There are, however, a few clues in Xántus's correspondence which indicate how he really felt about the issue of the conflict.

The motivation for his apolitical stance is best shown in a folder printed by Xántus in Washington on December 1, 1862, in defense of an attack on him by a countryman. The folder contained an account of his explorations as printed in the annual reports of the Smithsonian Institute for 1859 to 1861. In the preface, Xántus pleads:

During my residence of over ten years in the United States, I have always walked quietly along my path, minding my own business and not interfering with that of others. The sole object of my life has been to struggle up to a position where I could do something for our beloved homeland. I succeeded after toil and privation and sacrifices of comfort and material interests to present almost every scientific institute at home with specimens of American art, industry, and natural history. In quality as well as quantity, these surpass any and every collection in our Fatherland thus far.

In other words, Xántus here expresses the typical scientist's attitude of political noninvolvement. But a letter printed on September 18, 1862, in the *Györi Közlöny (Gazette of Győr)*, in which he described a trip from New York to Philadelphia, also contains a sharp attack on England for its aid to the Confederacy; a follow-up letter printed in the same journal on November 23, 1862, shows that Xántus devoted the entire message to listing the names of Hungarians who were serving in the Union Army, commending them lavishly. And finally, while employed in the surgeon-general's office in war-time Washington, he wrote Professor Baird in Carlisle, Pennsylvania, on August 29, 1862, complaining about the ineffectiveness of the army:

Our city very gloomy, the most extravagant rumors everywhere. One thing is certain: the enemy is this side of Fairfax. I can't understand how this can happen, we have so many resources, so many advantages over the Rebels, and still lose ground.... The world has never witnessed such a spectacle!

Whisky sellers, owners of beer houses, tailors, cigar makers, and so on, are now colonels, majors and captains!

These are the few clues we have that demonstrate his concern and also where his sympathies lay.

Notes

1. Xántus is discussing here the bighorn or Rocky Mountain sheep and the Rocky Mountain goat, which is not really a goat but looks like one. Xántus's assertion that the bighorn and Rocky Mountain goats found in the Rocky Mountains and the Sierra Nevadas as well as in northern Mexico (and Alaska as well) are not identical with their Asian counterparts is correct. But his theory that "not a single American mammal is identical with its Asian counterpart" is untenable. The land bridge between North America and northern Asia disappeared at a comparatively recent date. Since both regions are in the northern hemisphere with almost identical climates there is a great similarity between the mammals of both continents, with some notable exceptions. In addition to such species as the Rocky Mountain goat, which is not to be found elsewhere in the world, other species peculiar to North America and not found in Asia include the mountain lion, the jaguar, the gray fox, and the raccoon.

2. This reference is puzzling because Dr. Wagner never wrote a book under this title and he never visited the Tejon Islands. A possible explanation could be that Wagner and Scherzer turned down Xántus's offer in 1853 for a joint expedition to Central America and Xántus may be expressing a grudge in this childish way.

3. Xántus's observations and comments apply to the activities of General Edward F. Beale, who was appointed Superintendent of Indian Affairs for California in 1852. Beale advocated the establishment of mission-style reservations where Indians would gather and be instructed under the watchful eye of an agent and nearby soldiers. Beale concentrated his efforts on Rancho El Tejon. The Tejon reservation, on which he spent large federal funds, was a complete failure because the site was a poor choice. It could never have supported a population of 2,500 as planned, and it had white claimants. The recipients of a Mexican grant of 1843 were never bought out. Beale was succeeded in 1854 when the U.S. army post Fort Tejon was established. Later, Beale became the owner of Rancho Tejon and encouraged the Indians to remain, employing them as vaqueros and laborers. In spite of Beale's humane treatment, by 1858 Tejon and other posts were described as "almshouses for a trifling number of Indians" and the summary of J. Ross Browne, the famous Treasury agent of the 1850s is quite clear:

The results of the BIA policy pursued were such as might have been expected. A very large amount of money was expended annually in feeding white men and starving Indians. . . . In the brief period of six years they have been nearly destroyed by the . . . government. What neglect, starvation, and disease have not done, has been achieved by the cooperation of the white settlers in the great work of extermination. [J. Ross Browne, *The California Indians*, undated pamphlet.]

There is a curious reference by Xántus to an encounter with the then Lieutenant Beale. In a letter to Professor Baird dated February 2, 1858, he says: "I have to inform you again of a great calamity. Lieutenant Beale started out for here several days ago with his camels and, having no escort, he enlisted citizens and armed them from the ordnance store of this post. Consequently he took every musket, carbine, pistol, and saber on hand. And I am now entirely naked (scientifically speaking!)."

It is somewhat puzzling that Xántus does not elaborate on the extraordinary experiment in transportation initiated by Beale, who was the first to bring the news of the California gold strike east. The discovery of gold at Sutter's Creek made urgent the need for a wagon road across the southwestern desert of New Mexico and Arizona. But the desert devoured horses and mules. Beale had suggested using camels and Congress agreed. In 1855 it appropriated $30,000 to import seventy-seven camels and dromedaries, and in 1857 Lieutenant Beale led the unique camel expedition across the desert to his ranch at Fort Tejon.

Bibliography

Cholnoky, Eugene. "In Memory of John Xantus." *Bulletin of the Hungarian Geographic Society.* Budapest, 1925. Pp. 210–12.

Dictionary of American Biography. s.v. "Xantus, János."

Essig, Edward Oliver. *A History of Entomology.* New York: Macmillan, 1931.

György, Aladár. "Xantus János." *Bulletin of the Hungarian Geographic Society.* Budapest, 1894. Pp. 377–81.

Harris, Harry. "Notes on the Xantus Tradition." *Condor* 36 (1934): 191–201.

Hume, Edgar Erskine. *Ornithologists of the United States Army Medical Corps: Thirty-six Biographies.* Baltimore: Johns Hopkins Press, 1942.

Lantos, Louis. "John Xantus: A Memorial." *Natural Science Bulletin* 67 (1935): 467–71.

Lengyel, Emil. *Americans from Hungary.* Philadelphia: Lippincott, 1948.

Madden, Henry Miller. *Xantus, Hungarian Naturalist in the Pioneer West.* Palo Alto, Cal.: Books of the West, 1949.

Mocsáry, Sándor. "In Memory of John Xantus: Eulogies." *Proceedings, Hungarian Academy of Science.* Budapest, 1899. Pp. 231–58.

Palmer, Theodore Sherman. "Notes on Persons Whose Names Appear in the Nomenclature of California Birds." *Condor* 30 (1928): 261–307.

Pivány, Eugene. *Hungarian-American Historical Connections.* Budapest, 1927.

Rodgers, Andrew Denny. *John Torrey: A Story of North American Botany.* Princeton, N.J.: Hafner, 1942.

Smithsonian Institution. *Annual Reports for the Years 1856–1864.*

Steinbeck, John, and Ricketts, Edward F. *Sea of Cortez.* New York: Viking Press, 1941.

Szinnyei, Joseph. *Lives and Works of Hungarian Writers.* Vol. 14. Budapest, 1914.

Index

John Xántus came to America before the Civil War as a refugee from Hungary, where he had participated in the unsuccessful revolution of 1848. In the mid-1850s he traveled across America to California, where he began the collection of plants and animal life that was to make him a distinguished figure among the world's natural scientists.

Travels in Southern California is the second translation of a Xántus work by Theodore Schoenman and Helen Benedek Schoenman. Their earlier translation of his Letters from North America was published by the Wayne State University Press in 1975.

Mr. and Mrs. Schoenman have for years pursued an interest in the writings of political refugees from the 1848 war for Hungarian independence who, like Xántus, came to America in the years preceding the Civil War. They are currently preparing a biography of Agoston Haraszthy, founder of the California wine industry, and translating his Travels in North America (Pest, 1844). Forthcoming from the American Philosophical Society, Philadelphia, is their critical essay and translation of Journey in North America (Pest, 1834) by Alexander de Bölön Farkas, whose glowing tributes to American democracy helped trigger the Hungarian revolution and inspired the flight of many political activists to our shores.

The manuscript was prepared for publication by Elaine P. Halperin. The book was designed by Julie Paul. The typeface for the text is Caledonia designed by W. A. Dwiggins about 1938; and the display face is Caslon Old Style with swash caps based on the original design by William Caslon in the eighteenth century.

The text is printed on EB Booknatural paper, and the book is bound in Columbia Mills Fictionette cloth over binders boards. Manufactured in the United States of America.

Date Due